LEAVENWORTH SEVEN

LEAVENWORTH SEVEN

The Deadly 1931 Prison Break

KENNETH M. LAMASTER

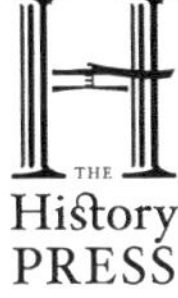

Published by The History Press
Charleston, SC
www.historypress.com

Front cover, top (left to right): George Curtis, Tom Underwood, Stanley Brown. *Courtesy of the author*; *bottom*: Front elevation, USP Leavenworth. *Courtesy of the author.*
Back cover, top: Aerial view, USP Leavenworth, 1931. *Courtesy of the author*; *inset*: The last ride of the Leavenworth Seven. *Courtesy of the author.*

First published 2019

Manufactured in the United States

ISBN 9781467140409

Library of Congress Control Number: 2018960975

Notice: The information in this book is true and complete to the best of our knowledge. It is offered without guarantee on the part of the author or The History Press. The author and The History Press disclaim all liability in connection with the use of this book.

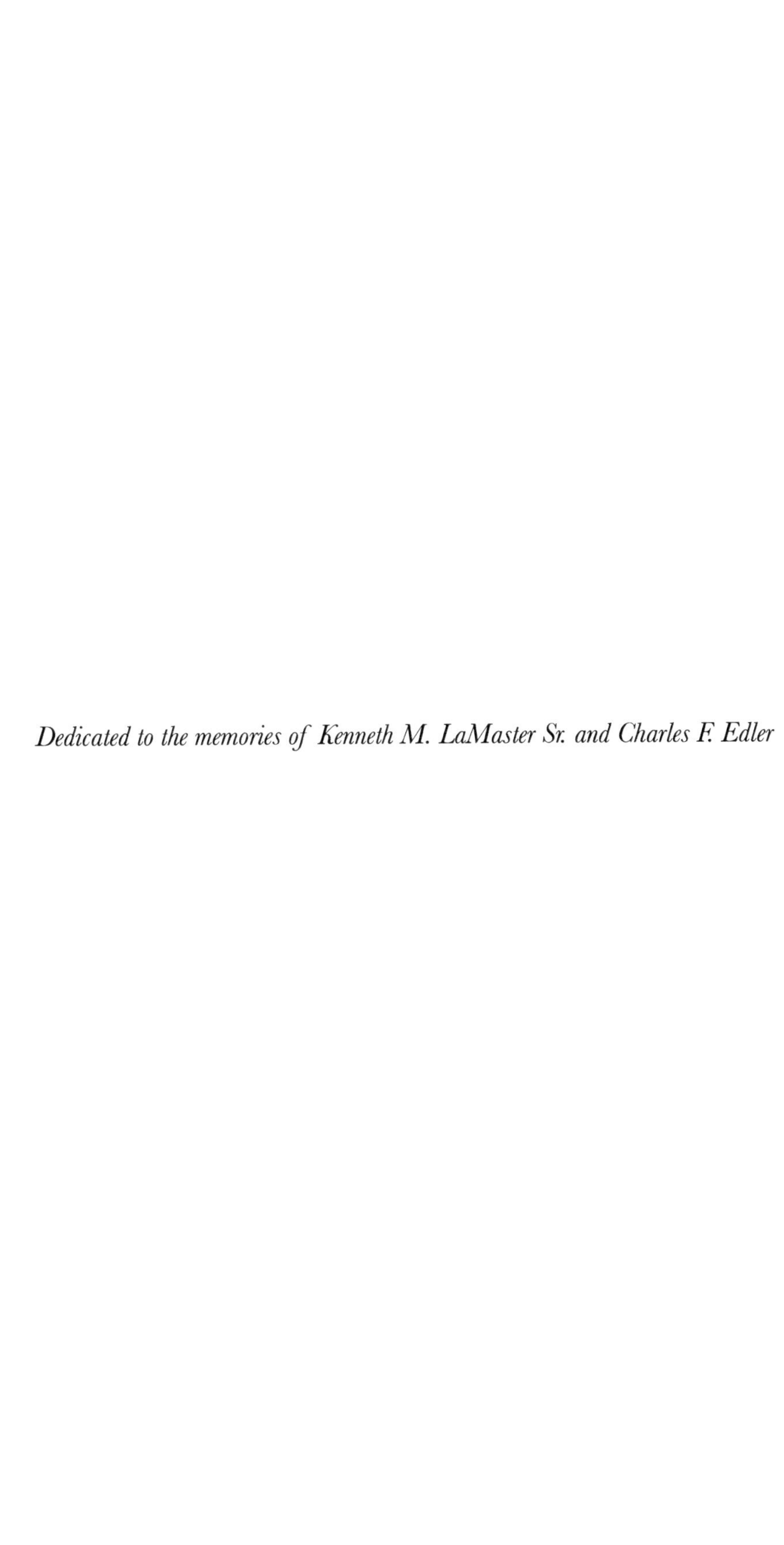

Dedicated to the memories of Kenneth M. LaMaster Sr. and Charles F. Edler

CONTENTS

PREFACE

My career began at the United States Penitentiary in Leavenworth, Kansas, on July 24, 1983. Just as with everyone else who had gone before me, my first days were filled with countless pages of forms ranging from insurance to emergency locator information, taking the usual physical and then being issued my first official Federal Bureau of Prisons I.D. card. That day, we were introduced to the person who was to guide us through institution familiarization training. For the next few weeks, Bobby Lawrence showed us the ways of being the best correctional officers we could be. His was the daunting task of teaching us the policies and procedures that would help us succeed. Along the way, Bobby gave us a brief overview of the institution's history.

It was during this overview that I first learned of the December 11, 1931 escape that I am presenting here. As the story goes, countless bureau policies have been instituted as a result of that escape. First and foremost, if anyone from the warden on down is taken hostage and brought to the gate and the inmates demand to be released, it is to be understood that the gates will not be opened and that those persons being held hostage have no power or authority whatsoever to give orders. If at that point the hostage-takers were to threaten to kill the hostages, we were instructed to refuse to open any gate and walk away from the control panel that opens the doors to freedom. Simply walking away would eliminate the possibility of a person's sympathies for the hostages leading to the release of the inmates. It also insured that the officer in control of the gate could not be a witness if the inmates carried out the threat and killed a hostage.

From the moment the discussion began about the 1931 escape, I became intrigued. Many questions began swirling through my head. Every opportunity I had afterward, I would track down newspaper accounts, magazine articles and any old-time Leavenworth staff members who could relate any information about the escape. For the remainder of my career, which spanned twenty-seven years, I spent countless and sometimes exhaustive hours reading and searching for anything that could tell me the story of that day. Along the way, I have amassed a collection of photographs, articles, inmate files, artifacts and even 2,500 pages of FBI reports that opened the door to the entire story. I have made countless acquaintances from the National Archives and historical societies in Illinois, Oklahoma, Kansas and California. At times, it has appeared that I have been guided in the direction I needed to go when I ran into a brick wall. One such occurrence came when I was talking to my father-in-law about how it would be great if I could find photographs to include with the telling of this story. The next morning, I was on the computer searching eBay for Leavenworth memorabilia when I came across several auctions that included Hearst news agency pictures covering the escape about which I am writing. Those are contained within this book.

Anyone who has worked in a correctional facility can tell you that the threat of an escape is constant. Many times over the course of a career, more escapes are broken up than actually occur. Many times, it's a snitch who brings the plot to the staff's attention. Officers have stumbled upon hidden contraband that was to be used in an attempt, and many times this discovery leads right to the cell doors of the escapees. Less often does an escape occur during which inmates take hostages with the idea of forcing their way to freedom. But during the 1920s and 1930s, a lawlessness prevailed, and desperate men resorted to desperate measures.

On May 30, 1933, a few miles south of the Leavenworth Federal Prison, inmates at the Kansas State Penitentiary are enjoying a Memorial Day watching a baseball game on the yard. Warden Kirk Prather suddenly realizes that he has been surrounded by some of the prison's more notorious criminals. As Prather began to move, he was confronted by six inmates armed with semiautomatic pistols. Eleven inmates, including Harvey J. Bailey and Wilbur "the Tri-State Terror" Underhill, manage to take Prather and fourteen officers hostage. As they make their way toward the southeast corner of the institution, the warden is issued an ultimatum: order the tower officer to throw down the keys to the tower's entry door or the inmates would open fire, killing the hostages. As the entrance to the tower opened, the inmates forced Prather and two officers up the stairs. Once they reached the observation deck of the tower, one inmate produces a rope, and the eleven inmates, the warden and two officers (taken as hostages) lower themselves to the ground and make their way into two waiting getaway cars.[1]

On September 26, 1933, associates of John Dillinger—namely Harry "Pete" Pierpont, Charles Mackey and John "Red" Hamilton, along with eight others—began luring staff into a trap in the basement of the prison shirt factory at the Indiana State Penitentiary at Michigan City. Using pistols that had been smuggled into the prison by the recently paroled Dillinger, the eleven desperate men made their way across the prison compound and through three gates to freedom. Along the way, they took numerous hostages. Deputy Superintendent Albert Evans and Officer Fred Willintz were severely beaten, and seventy-two-year-old Finley Carson was shot twice for moving too slow. Unlike in the movie *Public Enemies*, once the last door was open, it was virtually every man for himself. Dillinger had been arrested four days earlier and was being held in the Lima (Ohio) County Jail on a charge of bank robbery.[2]

On January 13, 1934, Floyd Hamilton and Jimmy Mullens made their way through the barbed wire fence along the outer edges of the Texas State Prison Farm in Eastham.[3] Their goal was to hide two Colt .45 pistols and several loaded magazines concealed in an inner tube just inside a culvert. On the morning of January 16, inmate work crews began clearing debris in preparation for the spring planting. Guarded by a "long arm man" mounted on horseback at a distance with a high-powered rifle, the inmates go about their work. As the inmates left the prison, Officer Olan Bozeman noticed that Hamilton's younger brother Raymond had jumped squads and was working with a detail on which he didn't belong. Once on the jobsite, Bozeman motions for the long arm man, Officer Major Crowson. As the two officers converse about what to do with Hamilton, inmate Joe Palmer approaches them to ask a question. Suddenly, Palmer produces one of the weapons and tells the officers, "sit still, don't move and there will be no shooting." Seconds later, a shot rings out, and a mortally wounded Crowson mounts his horse and rides toward the prison. Bozeman engages Hamilton in a gun battle that results in the officer being struck in the hip. From out of nowhere, responding officers are stopped in their tracks as they fall victim to a heavy barrage of automatic rifle fire. Concealed along the banks of a river to the south, Clyde Barrow, who has sworn vengeance upon all who work at Eastham, is laying down a hail of bullets that sends officers and inmates alike scrambling. Hamilton, Palmer, Henry Methvin and Hilton Bybee make their way to a waiting car driven by Bonnie Parker.[4]

Each of these escapes, though different, show how desperate men can be and how fast a routine day at a prison can erode into chaos within seconds. They also bear a striking similarity to the story you are about to read. The events of December 11, 1931, are eerily similar and were covered in virtually every news medium of that era. All of these escapes involved weapons smuggled into the prison, hostages and violence.

I write this story not only as an article of historical significance regarding what truly happened on that day long ago, I also write it to pay tribute to those who endured the experiences of being a hostage or a witness to the violence and to those who suffered injury and to the federal prison officers, county sheriffs and military and civilian posse members who relentlessly, without regard for personal safety, came together while facing terrific peril.

I would also like to thank those who have aided me in my research along the way: Mary Alice Hund for supplying me with the recollections of Rose Haas Frietchen; Herbert and Genevieve Schwinn; Richard Ochs Monica Fink and Rosemond Mayer Hendricks; the staff of the Leavenworth Public Library; the *Leavenworth Times*; the National Archives and Records Administration staff in Kansas City and San Bruno, California; the Oklahoma Historical Society; the Texas Ranger Hall of Fame and Museum and the Abraham Lincoln Presidential Library and Museum.

Most of all, I would like to express my gratitude to you, the reader. I hope you enjoy reading this story as I have enjoyed writing it.

1

ESCAPED!

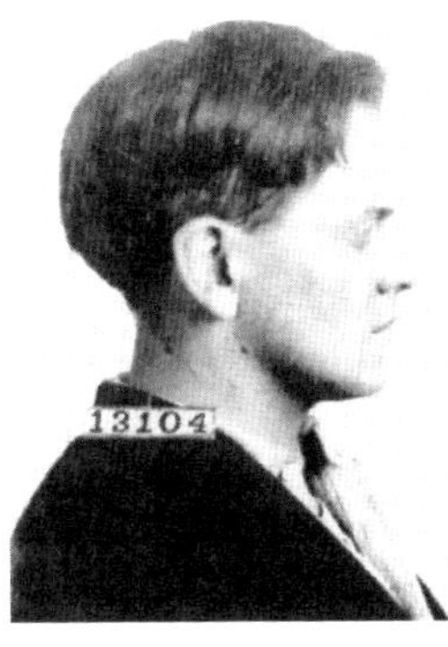

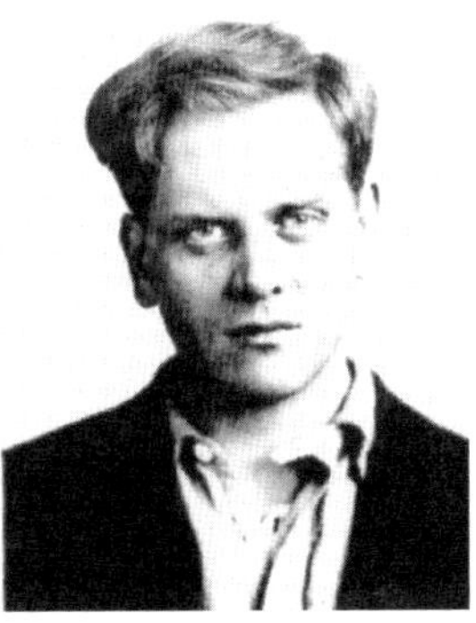

Ralph H. Chaplin. *Courtesy National Archives and Records Administration.*

(The boiler-house whistle is blown "wildcat" when
A prisoner makes a "getaway")
A MAN has fled…! We clutch the bars and
Wait;
The corridors are empty, tense and still;
A silver mist has dimmed the distant hill;
The guards have gathered at the prison gate.
Then suddenly the "wildcat" blares its hate
Like some mad Moloch screaming for the kill.
Shattering the air with terror loud and shrill.
The dim, grey walls become articulate.

Freedom, you say? Behold her altar here!
In those far cities men can only find
A vaster prison and a redder hell,
Overshadowed by new wings of greater fear.
Brave fool, for such a world to leave behind
The iron sanctuary of a cell! [5]

Ralph H. Chaplin, USP Leavenworth Inmate No. 13104

2

THE BIG L: THE BEGINNING

Construction began on the United States Penitentiary at Leavenworth, Kansas, in March 1897. Since July 1895, federal prisoners had been housed in the old military prison located just three miles away at Fort Leavenworth. At dawn's first light, inmates marched from the fort to the new construction site in a military-style formation escorted by armed officers—some on horseback, others marching alongside. For seven days each week, 300 inmates, 17 teams of mules and 30 staff made the journey. Whether undertaken in blistering heat, driving rain or deep snow, theirs was a daunting task of man against the elements.

From day one, inmates devised plans of escape. Many would find it easy enough to just walk away unnoticed. Inmate George East, a horse thief, attempted to walk away and was ordered to halt. Upon hearing this command, poor old George was prompted to run and was met with a volley of gunfire that led to his untimely demise. Many others were captured by locals and returned. For these indiscretions, inmates received harsh punishments. A reduction in grade and being placed into stripes were the most common. For those who seemed willing to run at any given moment, they were tasked with wearing a ball and chain—a fifteen-pound cannon shot welded to a piece of iron chain with a shackle that, once placed around the ankle, was hot-riveted by the blacksmith. If this were not bad enough, these inmates were still required to fall out for morning formation and make the trip to the construction site. Once there, these inmates would spend the entire day walking the perimeter of the fence that surrounded the seventeen-acre compound. Their fellow inmates soon dubbed this "carrying the baby."

Inmates were tasked with building the new institution using crude everyday hand tools such as picks and shovels. A quarry was dug west of the institution site and provided the stone for the foundations of the buildings. The leveling of the site was done by hand, and the trenches for the foundations of buildings were all hand-dug. This provided the clay for the on-site brick factory. A small rail system with a small steam locomotive was built so materials could be moved about the site. To prevent inmates from escaping, a perimeter fence was constructed. As a further deterrent, the foundation for the wall was dug forty feet below the surface. As the stone was delivered for the foundations, a steam winch was constructed that lifted the stone into the hole, where inmates would then muscle it into place.[6]

The first official escape at the Big L occurred on the morning of June 1, 1898. A detail of eighty-one inmates had just arrived at the construction site along with their escorting officers Henry Duffy and A.W. Earnest. As the detail was entering the perimeter gate, Officer Bruce King was climbing the ladder leading to the tower overlooking the gate. Earnest and Duffy's orders were to stand at a distance of thirty feet, with one in front and to the side with the other to the rear and on the opposite side of the formation. Both were to stand with their revolvers in hand until all six towers were manned and ready.

On this particular morning, Duffy was standing in front of the formation with Earnest standing toward the rear. As King was climbing the ladder to the tower, Duffy, with his pistol holstered, walked past the front of the formation within ten feet and took the holstered weapon of Earnest and again passed within ten feet of the inmates with his back to the formation. Without warning or hesitation, inmates William Pearce, John Adams, William Werth and Ulysses Ritter attacked Duffy from behind. As Earnest responded to the aid of his fellow officer, he was attacked. Both officers were overwhelmed and thrown to the ground. Once they were on the ground, the pistols were wrestled away from Duffy, and as he lay there, inmate Pearce cocked the hammer and pointed one of the pistols at him.

"I would rather this pistol was in any hands except yours!" exclaimed Pearce. "Do as you're told and you won't get hurt!" A group of inmates jerked the officer from the ground and marched toward the gate. Once there, another group of inmates congregated under the tower with Officer Earnest. As Officer King reached the top of the tower, he heard the commotion

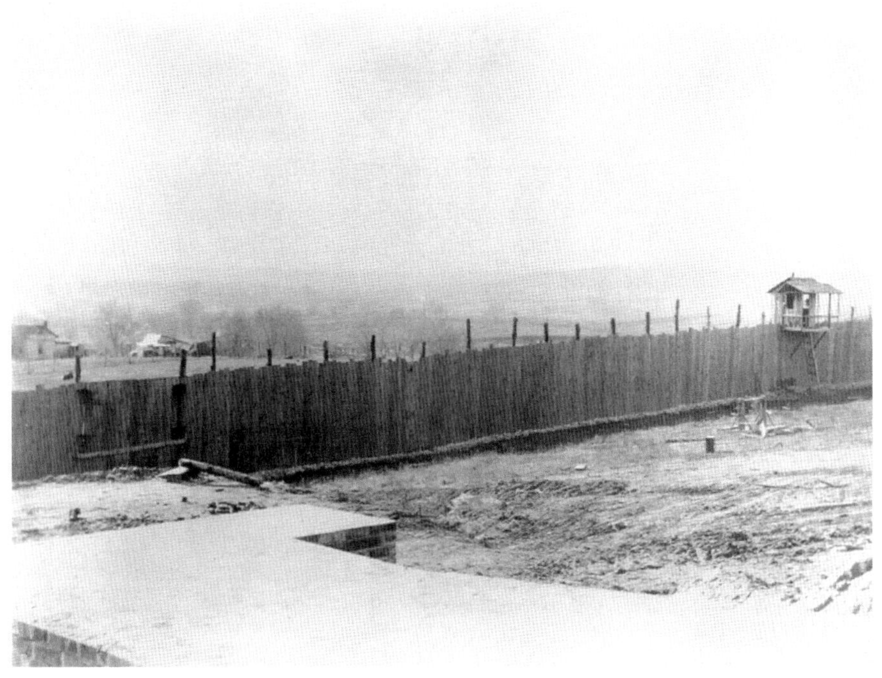

Early construction photo of the west wall. It was along this wooden perimeter where inmates gathered hostages and made their escape on November 7, 1901. *Courtesy of the author.*

below, and as he peered out the window, he heard, "God damn it, King, come on out of that tower and throw down that gun!" Realizing the inmates were using the officers as human shields, King exited the tower and held his rifle over the rail. Duffy began to shake his head silently, telling King "no." One of the inmates, who was armed with an iron bar, raised it over Duffy's head, and another was screaming, "Kill him, God damn him, if he don't stop shaking his head!" King dropped the rifle as both officers were forced toward and through the gate. Fewer than a dozen inmates participated in the escape, and all but Pearce and Ritter were recaptured within minutes. Both officers were released unharmed.

Pearce, who had been sent to Leavenworth for housebreaking and the robbing of several post offices, remained free. With a sixty-dollar bounty on his head, he was captured in July 1903 in Wyoming during the robbery of—what else—a post office. After serving time in the state penitentiary for the robbery, Pearce was returned to Leavenworth to complete his sentence.[7] Ritter somehow eluded capture and would never again call Leavenworth home. His name remained on the list of inmates who had escaped and never returned well into the 1960s. Anyone who had been on escape status and reached the age of 75 was presumed to be deceased. These lists are no longer produced by the Bureau of Prisons.

As with any escape that has ever occurred, someone is going to face the blame. Amongst staff of the Federal Bureau of Prisons, this has become known as being in the penalty box. Many times, even though officers may be suspended or relieved of duty, wardens and other executive staff will come under fire as well. In his official report of the June 1, 1898 escape, Warden J.W. French, who had come under fire from U.S. attorney general John W. Griggs, responded, "I insist that if a warden has required of a subordinate no unreasonable thing, if he has properly instructed the subordinate and dispatched him in the line of duty, the warden is not at fault." Warden French also advised that he would have fired both officers, but due to staffing levels at the construction site being inadequate, he had moved them to less responsible positions, stating, "I am without authority to do more than suspend. I believe it would be to the good of the service to permanently relieve them from the guard and I so recommend."

The staffing levels at the construction site often pitted the supervisor of construction, F.E. Hinds, against the warden. In his reports, Hinds often wrote of delays due to an unskilled labor force and French's policy of allowing a tobacco break every couple of hours. After the noon meal, every inmate and officer was subjected to close-order drilling, and officers were even required to read the Bible to inmates for a period of one hour.

French, who had been appointed to his position by Democratic president Grover Cleveland in 1895, had petitioned the government to include the positions of wardens and correctional officers under the Civil Service Act, which had been established in 1883. Local Republicans saw this as an attempt by French to secure his position—as well as those of his staff—should a Republican be elected to the presidency. Serious accusations were made that the officers could be seen nightly getting drunk, frequenting houses of prostitution, gambling and reporting for work the next morning unfit to perform their duties.

The executive staff and officers of the nearby Kansas State Penitentiary had even accused French of favoritism in hiring as well as allowing his deputy warden and staff to enter public places and openly campaign for the reelection of Cleveland during the 1896 election. In some instances, it was reported that the officers had resorted to brawling with the locals over their difference in candidates and that such behavior had gone unpunished and was encouraged. Succumbing to these accusations, French resigned his position and was replaced on July 1, 1899.

Major Robert W. McClaughry had risen to prominence during his service with the 118th Illinois Volunteer Infantry during the Civil War. Afterward, he gained even greater prominence as a prison reformer during his stints as warden of the Illinois State Penitentiary and Pennsylvania Industrial Reformatory, Chicago chief of police and superintendent of the Illinois State Reformatory. He believed in the remedial, not retributive, treatment of prisoners. McClaughry, a staunch Republican whose loyalty dated back to his days campaigning for the election of Abraham Lincoln, was appointed to the position of warden by President William McKinley.

From the very moment the new warden took over, things began to change. Inmates and officers were issued a book of rules to which all were expected to adhere. No longer would inmates be allowed the use of tobacco, and there would be no close-order drilling. Inmates were also prohibited from speaking to each other. Work at the construction site would be reduced to six days per week, but officers were required to work the full seven. Officers were no longer required to read the Bible to inmates. If officers required a day off, they would have to find their own replacements, and only the warden could approve the time off. Officers were also required to address each other as "mister" accompanied by last name, even if they were related. A deputy warden was appointed to ensure officers were not visiting local gambling houses, brothels or saloons during their off-duty hours. There would be no boisterous laughter, spirited conversations of politics nor scuffling of the feet. Officers would now address the inmates by their numbers only—no names.

Also prohibited was addressing inmates by nicknames such as Shorty, Fatty, Lefty, Frenchie or any name distinguished by any deformity, characteristic, nationality or ethnicity. Weekly firearms training for officers would be mandatory and conducted in full view of the inmates. For the first time, officers would be appointed in accordance to prior military or law enforcement experience. It was to be fully understood that officers would conduct themselves professionally and treat inmates in a firm but fair manner. Any divergence from these rules would result in swift punishment.

As work continued on the new facility, the *Leavenworth Times* reported that trainloads of curious onlookers were arriving from Kansas City, as well as other areas around the Midwest, to make a day out of watching the progress. Camping out along Metropolitan Avenue with picnic baskets took on a carnival-like atmosphere, with kids and adults playing, photographers snapping pictures and hucksters hawking everything from postcards and picture books to porcelain cups and saucers and silver spoons. Warden McClaughry felt it was his duty to personally escort visiting dignitaries at the construction site. He also felt that since the facility was being built with taxpayers' dollars, anyone who wished to tour the site would be accommodated. These tours would be handled by the deputy warden or captain of the guard. Officers and inmates alike understood that they were to continue work as the tours were conducted with strict orders to not look at or appear to be gawking at visitors. Officers were not allowed to speak with visitors unless asked a question. Inmates were prohibited any contact of any type.

Over the next few years, construction continued and progressed at a much faster pace. The outline of the first cell house, dining room and kitchen area sprang up. Buildings such as the current day laundry building and powerhouse, along with the west wall, provided a better understanding as to how the finished institution would look. For the most part, construction was ahead of schedule. Also noted was the decrease in inmate escapes. Those who did escape would still be reduced to wearing stripes and ball and chain, but they would no longer "carry the baby." Malcontents would be returned to their details to work alongside their fellow inmates.

After the ball and chain were removed, they were introduced to a new device that limited their ability to run: the Gardner Shackle (also known by its more common name, the Oregon Boot). This device consisted of an iron brace that would be fixed around the heel of the inmate's boot. Then, a piece of iron weighing between five and twenty-eight pounds would be placed around the top of the boot and locked into place. This allowed the weight to be decreased over time with the inmate being required to sign a promissory letter that he would be good to be fully released from the device.

Two of the institution's most prominent escapes occurred during McClaughry's tenure. At about 8:30 a.m. on the morning of April 21, 1910, a Union Pacific engine approached the east gate of the institution and gave the usual signal that it had arrived with a load of lumber. As was customary during that time, trains loaded with supplies and incoming inmates passed through the east gate and were unloaded in the area located in front of the institution's powerhouse. This area was known as two gang alley—so named because the powerhouse required two gangs of inmates shoveling coal to insure the main boilers remained fired. On this particular morning, Captain Fred Zerbst and Officer Harry Reed escorted the train through the gates and proceeded to the scales area in front of the powerhouse. Zerbst proceeded to the scales as usual while Reed positioned himself near the engine tender. Suddenly, without warning, Reed was grabbed from behind by inmate Arthur Hewitt, who was clutching a pistol while inmate Frank Grigware wielded an ax. The inmates forced Reed upon the engine and were closely followed by four additional inmates. Hewitt, armed with the revolver, thrust the weapon into the face of the engineer, threatening to kill him if he didn't open the throttle and ram the west gate. Fearing for his life, the engineer obeyed the order and slammed through the west gate and out across the western edge of the institution. Within minutes, the inmates were forced to abandon the train when they came upon a construction crew working on the bridge crossing Salt Creek. Within hours, five of the six inmates were captured and returned to the institution. It was then discovered that the pistol used to effect the escape was in fact carved from wood. McClaughry's report[8] indicated that the revolver "was so well made it would deceive any ordinary observer." Grigware remained at large, making his way to Canada. In 1934, a man was arrested for trapping out of season and fingerprinted by Canadian authorities. The man, known by the name of Jim Fahey, was in fact Frank Grigware. He had lived an exemplary life and had even served as mayor of the town in which he resided. Canadian officials resisted countless appeals by the United States authorities calling for his extradition. Considered a model citizen, Grigware was allowed to live out his life as a free man.

The escape of 1910 would change the operation of the institution in that full-size train engines would no longer be allowed inside. A smaller engine was purchased by the institution, one that could tow supplies inside for unloading. The west gate was walled up, and an armory and pedestrian gate were installed. A few months prior to the escape, McClaughry had asked officials in Washington for modification to the west wall. His rationale was that he feared someone could commandeer the supply train and effect an escape by crashing it through.

Even though the escape of 1910 had an effect on the operation of the institution, it was the escape that had occurred nearly nine years earlier that would change not just the institution but the Federal Prison Service forever.

On the afternoon of November 7, 1901, inmates were finishing up the day's work and readying themselves for the march back to the old military prison.[9] At about 3:40 that afternoon, construction superintendent F.E. Hinds, tin shop foreman Herman H. Boehn and captain Arthur Telford were in the construction office when, suddenly, inmates Gus Parker, Thomas Kating and Bob Clark[10] slammed through the door, producing two revolvers. One of the inmates exclaimed, "We want you to throw yer hands up and get out here!" As the three hostages were forced out of the office, they could hear the phone being ripped from the wall and destroyed by Parker, who had armed himself with a hammer. Once outside, they encountered inmate Arthur Hewitt, who had armed himself with an iron bar. As the stonecutting foreman William F. Carroll was passing by, he was forced to join the three other hostages.

The inmates, using the hostages as human shields, approached the west gate tower pointing their revolvers at Officer John Hoffman and demanding that he put down his weapon and exit his tower. Hoffman took aim as superintendent Hinds threw up his hands and yelled, "Don't shoot, it would be murder!" Hoffman, who feared killing the hostages, laid down his weapon and came down from his tower. As he complied, inmates W.C. Murray, Frank Thompson and Parker forced their way past him and secured the weapons, which included several revolvers, shotguns and a Winchester rifle.

As the inmates forced open the gate along the west wall, they encountered a group of armed officers who had been supervising a detail outside the secure perimeter. Seizing the opportunity, Captain Telford forced his way clear of the hostage-takers and through the gate. As he made his way toward the tower along the northwest corner, inmate Kating opened fire, hitting Telford in the leg. Officer Sullivan, who was stationed in the northwest tower, was taking up a defensive position when he suddenly came under a barrage of gunfire. Officer Andrew Leonard, who had been supervising a crew laying brick atop the west wall, witnessed what was happening and, in an attempt to warn others, leaped from the scaffolding onto a pile of bricks. As Leonard lay there with a broken leg, inmate Frank Thompson, who had exited the tower, spun and cocked the hammer of his revolver. As he pointed it at the head of Officer Leonard, one of the other hostage-takers exclaimed, "You can't shoot an unarmed man!" Thompson hesitated, then laughed as he ran south toward the main gate of the construction site. Amid the growing chaos, inmate J.J. Poffenholtz, who had armed himself with a revolver, was seen aimlessly wandering about the site and crying.

After slamming the gate shut, the growing number of inmates, even more determined, made their way south along the west wall. Inmate Thompson had taken up a position along the southeast corner of the laundry building and opened fire on the tower of Officer J.B. Waldrupe, which was located on the southwest corner of the main gate. Officer C.E. Burrows, who was located on the gate tower opposite Waldrupe, attempted to open fire on Thompson, and as he pulled the trigger, his rifle misfired. Inmate Grayson fired upon Officer Burrows, striking him twice: one bullet hit him in the neck, while the other clipped off a piece of the officer's ear.

Inmates Kating, Hewitt and Clark, along with their hostages and an ever-increasing throng of inmates, approached the tower where Officer Waldrupe was located. The tower had come under a relentless hail of gunfire from Thompson and Grayson. As he fired upon the advancing mob, Waldrupe was struck in the right thigh by a bullet and fell to the floor. The officer regained his composure and returned fire, striking inmate Quinn Fort in the head and instantly killing him. Almost as instantly, Waldrupe was struck right between the eyes by pellets from a shotgun blast. As the inmates turned their attention to the next tower, they saw the officer leap from the tower and set up a defensive position outside the perimeter as he was being joined by other armed officers. In an attempt to gather more weapons, inmate Don Sutherland began climbing up the ladder to Waldrupe's tower when, suddenly, the wounded officer fired his revolver downward and struck Sutherland, who immediately fell to the ground. Seeing the growing number of armed officers, inmates began tearing away at the plank wall that formed the perimeter of the gate. As the planks gave way, the inmates began exiting and running toward the southwest and to freedom.

Of the 380 inmates working at the construction site, only 26 had successfully escaped. During the chaos, officers were able to arm themselves and lay down a barrage of gunfire of their own. Within seconds, over one hundred shots had been fired inside the secure perimeter. As the mutiny escalated, the officers dispatched one of the young mule skinners to search for a phone. After arriving at the home of Jake Biddle, they placed calls to the military prison, garrison commander of Fort Leavenworth and the local authorities. A small detachment of infantry soldiers who had been nearby responded to the construction site. Upon arriving at the scene, Major Jacob Augur made his way to the construction office. There, he found the destroyed phone as well as Officer Leonard tending to his broken leg. J.B. Waldrupe, who was writhing in pain, was removed by ambulance to Saint John Hospital.

Officers started ordering the remaining inmates into formation. Major Augur had made his way to the formation as the detachment from the fort arrived. Four officers who had been able to pursue and capture six of the escapees arrived as well. The remaining inmates were refusing orders from the officers to form up. Knowing that the military had no authority to pursue the escapees beyond the grounds of the construction site, Major Augur brought the inmates under control when he issued the order, "First man gets out of line, shoot him!" The inmates immediately fell into formation. The military detachment, along with a small group of officers, marched the inmates out of the gate and toward the old military prison. The remaining officers joined the pursuit.

Upon arriving at the construction site, Warden McClaughry, who had been attending the Conference of the National Prison Congress in Kansas City, was apprised of the situation by Deputy Warden Frank Lemon. He immediately dispatched telegrams to all the local law enforcement agencies as well as Washington with details of the escape. Over the course of the next several days, reports poured in from surrounding areas about inmates who had been apprehended.

One report from nearby Nortonville told the story of inmates being pursued by a posse of citizens. After barricading themselves inside a barn, five escapees came under a hail of endless gunfire. When the smoke had settled, two were wounded, two were dead and the fifth surrendered unharmed. As each day passed, more escapees were captured and returned. An investigation revealed that former inmate Charles Ennis had returned to the unguarded compound at night and placed the weapons around the construction site. To alert his accomplices that the weapons were in place, Ennis had tied white string to the phone poles along the path on which the inmates marched every day.

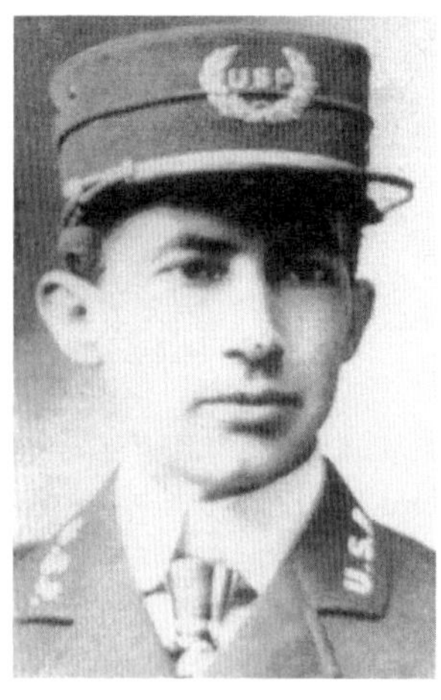

J.B. Waldrupe became the first officer to die in the line of duty for the Federal Prison Service. Upon hearing of his passing, Warden McClaughry declared, "Leavenworth is hell." *Courtesy Agnes T. Kramer.*

During the afternoon of November 9, exploratory surgery was performed on Officer Waldrupe. The bullet had entered the officer's forehead about a half-inch above the center point between both eyes and penetrated the skull approximately four and a half inches straight back. Though it penetrated the skull and settled at the base of the brain, the bullet never struck the brain. Word from the surgeon was that it was his belief the young officer would survive.

Word had spread throughout the community of the courageous battle of the young officer. Many had started a petition to have the young man awarded the Congressional Medal of Honor for his bravery. From the moment he arrived at the hospital, his wife of barely a year,

Lena, had remained by his side. Each day, the officer endured the probing of the injury, and each day, he appeared to be making a miraculous recovery. During the evening hours of November 15, Officer J.B. Waldrupe told his wife, Lena, that he felt well enough to set up. Soon afterward, he developed a fever and slipped into a coma. In the early morning hours of November 16, with his wife by his side, the young officer succumbed to his injuries.

Upon hearing of the death of Officer Waldrupe, Warden McClaughry was asked what sort of punishment those responsible would face once they were returned to the prison. McClaughry stoically replied, "Leavenworth is hell."

Within a month, all but one of the inmates had been captured, killed or returned to the facility. All were downgraded to third-grade striped uniforms, placed in shackles and put to work in the stone-breaking shed. As the investigation progressed, it was discovered that another escape plot was underway and was to take place on December 29.[11] Once again, inmates Gilbert Mullins, Frank Thompson and Bob Clark were the principal conspirators in a plan that now included inmates Turner Barnes and Frank Robeson. On that particular day, the four inmate barbers were to shave inmates working in the shed. At the appropriate time, a signal was to be given, and those involved were to seize the razors and overpower the officers. One inmate was to find Deputy Warden Lemon and tell him he was needed at the shed immediately. Upon arrival, the plan was to seize Lemon and then force their way toward the armory, where they would seize every weapon they could and make their way to the front gate and freedom. The plot also called for the killing of any officer who stood in their way.

The day before the escape, Warden McClaughry received word from another inmate who had overheard the plot. The warden, along with several officers, converged upon the shed and conducted a thorough search of the area and the inmates. A file (used to remove the shackles) was discovered, and a couple of sharpened case knives were found upon the persons of numerous inmates. Making good on his comment, McClaughry ordered the inmates stripped, placed in solitary confinement, shackled to the doors of the cells in the standing position and placed on a diet of bread and water. For all involved, Leavenworth would be hell.

3

NASH AND THE BOYS

Throughout the 1920s, newspapers and law enforcement agencies—namely, the FBI—made several outlaws infamous. Hardly a day passed that stories of Bonnie and Clyde, John Dillinger, Machine Gun Kelly and a host of others didn't make the front-page news. Ma Barker and her boys—Alvin "Creepy" Karpis, Pretty Boy Floyd and Baby Face Nelson—were immortalized by the nicknames they acquired (deservedly or not). As the years stretched into decades, many of them were immortalized in books, magazines and movies.

Mention the names Grover C. Durrill, George "Whitey" Fallon, Will "Boxcar" Green, Charles Berta, Tom Underwood, Earl Thayer or Stanley Brown, and no one remembers who they were; same with the names Thomas James Holden, Francis Keating or Harold Fontaine. In fact, mention the name Frank Nash, and most only remember him as a footnote to the Kansas City Union Station Massacre. None of these men became household names, but all were just as dangerous as (or even more dangerous than) those who garnered the most notoriety.

From the very moment the front gate swung open on July 1, 1895, and the first United States Penitentiary was opened for business, a myriad of criminals from all walks of life have made their way to Leavenworth, Kansas. Its cellblocks have housed some of the most notorious malefactors in the country's criminal history. From gangsters to bank robbers to drug dealers and international terrorists—and yes, even a few celebrities, USP Leavenworth has seen them all. It has also been home to one of the most professional groups of correctional professionals ever assembled. Through the years, the Leavenworth "hack" has dealt with them all.

If you're asking yourself what hack means, let me explain. Every prison has its inmate term or nickname for correctional officers. Boss, screw or cop may be familiar to most. The term boss, for example, is a reverse acronym—"Stupid Son of a Bitch"—that inmates devised not to show respect but for what they saw as humor. The term "hack," on the other hand, not only shows an inmate's disdain for the officer but shows some respect as well. Hack, or "Hard Ass Carrying Keys," recognizes the fair but firm approach developed over the years of dealing with the worst of the worst. USP Leavenworth was home to innovators of correctional techniques used all over the world. The institution housed the Bureau of Criminal Identification before the FBI, and it also served as the Bureau of Prisons' training grounds for new officers. The BOP's philosophy was to teach the "Leavenworth way."

By the time Frank Nash entered the front gates of Leavenworth, he had built quite a reputation as a skilled planner of criminal exploits.[12] Having grown up working in his father's hotel, he had also garnered the skill of talking to people. Nash's first conviction came in 1913, when he received a life sentence for the murder of Nollie "Humpy" Wortman. During the court proceedings, Nash was able to con jailers into allowing him to come and go from the jail late at night. One such instance led to Nash finding out the location of the prosecution's main witness, Maggie Lonnergan. Nash was able to abduct and hide her until after the trial. Though he had been successful in his attempt to regain freedom by hiding the witness, the prosecutors were allowed to use her statement from the pretrial proceeding to convict.

Upon arrival at the Oklahoma State Penitentiary at McAlester, Nash became a model inmate. A petition had been started on his behalf by Nash's friends around the Hobart area. Many couldn't believe that such a nice man could be involved in such a heinous act. While at McAlester, Nash developed "tuberculosis." Purportedly, his prison records indicated that he had been working as a hospital orderly and that the only medical treatment he had received during that time was having his appendix removed. No doubt Nash was able to build a rapport with the institution's doctor, who released a statement stating that Nash could not possibly receive proper treatment for the disease while incarcerated. Many prominent civic and political leaders took up Nash's cause, and on March 28, 1918, his sentence was commuted to ten years.

As the United States' involvement in World War I was increasing, governors and prosecutors began offering criminals a chance of a lifetime. If they agreed to enlist in the military and returned from the war and were released from military service with an honorable discharge, they would, in turn, receive a full pardon. Nash's prayers had been answered, and after talking with the warden, Nash was paroled with the stipulation that he enlist. In July 1918, Nash, along with other volunteers from Kiowa County, boarded a troop train headed for Camp Cody in Demming, New Mexico.

After serving a stint in France during the waning days of the war, Nash returned to Hobart, and it wasn't long afterward that he went back to his old ways. Bootlegging in the Osage Hills had always been a big business. Traveling throughout the region distributing illegal spirits afforded Nash the luxury of doing business with the likes of John Callahan, known far and wide as the best fence in the Midwest. Al Spencer, Wilber Underhill, Pretty Boy Floyd, Alvin "Creepy" Karpis, Eddie Adams and Diamond Joe Sullivan all became more than just acquaintances of Nash. It wasn't long before Nash graduated to the big time—robbing banks.

On the night of October 18, 1919, Frank Nash, along with George Meyers and Eddie Wade, pulled their first bank heist in the small farming community of Corn, Oklahoma. Unfortunately for them, their foray into the robbing business netted them a few hundred dollars in government bonds and $20 in pennies. Their attempt at blowing the safe open did nothing more than awaken a slumbering town and turn them all into witnesses. As the town began spreading the alarm, the trio escaped in a sedan, making it 120 miles away to the town of Chickasha, where they holed up at the Early Hotel. Later that day, while awaiting the ferry to take them across the South Canadian River at Tuttle, Nash and his fellow malefactors were taken into custody. Upon inspection of the car, a lawman found the bonds and other papers hidden in the upholstery. Evidence collected included $550 in Liberty Bonds, $708 in war savings stamps and $4.75 in savings stamps. On August 4, 1920, all three were sentenced to twenty-five years. Nash was on his way back to McAlester.

Once back in prison, Nash met up with his old friend Henry Starr and struck up a friendship with Al Spencer. Starr's career as an outlaw had begun in the early 1890s, and his expertise was as a horse thief and train robber. In December 1892, Starr was convicted of murder in the death of deputy U.S. marshal Floyd Wilson. He was tried twice for the murder by judge Isaac Parker but escaped hanging due to technicalities. Starr claimed ignorance of knowing Wilson was a U.S. marshal. Both convictions were overturned by the

U.S. Supreme Court. In January 1898, Starr pleaded guilty to manslaughter and received a fifteen-year sentence: three years for manslaughter, seven years for robbery and five years for train robbery. His sentence was reduced to five years by President Theodore Roosevelt, and Starr was released in January 1903. For the next ten years, Starr spent a short stint as an honest man until Arkansas officials learned of his release and began extradition proceedings to return him to Arkansas for trial in connection with the Bentonville Bank robbery of 1893. Then he went back to what he knew best, and for the next five years, Starr and his gang robbed banks in Kansas and Colorado. After a stint in the Canon City State Penitentiary that began in 1908 and lasted until 1913, Starr returned to Oklahoma and pulled off a total of fourteen bank robberies between September 1914 and January 1915. On March 27, 1915, Starr and his gang rode into Stroud, Oklahoma, and attempted to rob two banks simultaneously. Starr and another member of his gang were wounded in the ensuing gun battle and captured. On August 2, 1915, Henry Starr was sentenced to twenty-five years.

Unlike Starr, who loathed the media, Al Spencer loved every article ever written about him. Spencer fancied himself a modern Jesse James and had ridden with Starr during the Stroud bank robberies. Spencer, along with his brother-in-law Grover C. Durrill, had managed to escape and elude capture. Nash and Spencer became Starr's prize pupils, listening to every piece of advice the aging outlaw bestowed upon them. According to various accounts, Nash and Spencer spent this time planning for the day they'd be free to rob again. For Spencer, that day came on January 22, 1922, when the five-foot-six, one-hundred-and-thirty-pound outlaw affected his escape. Upon his return to the Osage Hills, he formed a new gang. Spencer's love of publicity caused the daring outlaw to be reckless, which led to the media's daily writings about his exploits.

Frank Nash, unlike his friends, preferred the much more pleasant method of leaving his confines. His ability to plan, scheme and con led to his release from McAlester on December 22, 1922. Once again, Nash had used his methods to convince the warden that he had been offered a position with a hay and grain firm and was granted a leave of absence for business reasons.

Upon his release, Nash became Spencer's chief lieutenant and planner. It was Nash's job to stake out the banks and plan the robberies. During the following months, Spencer and company racked up quite a few robberies and nearly three times the stories. The media reporting on his exploits dubbed Spencer the "King of the Bad Lands" or the "Wild Rider of the Osage

Hills." As word spread of Spencer's fondness for all the attention, the media began a crusade to bring down the gang. They began writing that he lacked the daring of the many outlaws he idolized such as the Daltons, Doolins and others. They chided Spencer for only robbing banks, usually for paltry sums, and his fear of robbing trains. It was Nash who had advised Spencer to stay away from train robbery; Nash's logic was that small-town banks were protected by local law officers, whereas railroad companies had huge staffs of railroad investigators, and if they were to steal mail pouches, that would also bring federal officers into the mix. Once on the trail of fugitives, railroad detectives and federal marshals were relentless in their pursuit and knew no boundaries.

The one and only time Spencer allowed the media to strike a negative chord forced him to go against Nash's advice. On the night of August 20, 1923, the Missouri, Kansas & Texas train known as the Katy Limited pulled into the station at Bartlesville loaded with $20,000 in Liberty Bonds en route from the Commercial National Bank in Muskogee and headed to the state treasurer's office in Oklahoma City. The plan[13] called for conspirator Ike Ogg to board the train in Bartlesville and request a special stop at the Okesa Station located fifteen miles west. Ogg abandoned this part of the plan when he learned that the section foreman, Charley Carson, had already planned to depart the train at the small flag stop.

At 12:10 a.m., the Katy Limited pulled out of the Bartlesville station. It was a warm summer's evening with not a cloud in the sky, and a bright moon cast a glow over the surrounding area. Covering the eleven miles in fifteen minutes, the train pulled into the depot at Okesa just long enough to drop Carson and began to pull away from the station. Fireman Byron D. Tower[14] was seated to the left of the engine's cab, and the train was barely underway when he noticed what appeared to be the silhouette of a man clinging to the top of the engine tender. As he turned around, he was confronted by Frank Nash and Grover C. Durrill as a pistol was jabbed hard into his side. Durrill ordered Tower to lay down on the floor, and as he complied, Durrill delivered a crashing blow to Tower's head with the butt of his pistol, rendering him unconscious for the next few minutes. Nash ordered engineer William C. Miller to bring the train to a complete stop. As the train came to a halt, Tower awakened a bloody mess from his head injury, and Durrill suddenly began kicking and ordering him to his feet and to climb down from the engine. As the two men reached the area between the baggage car and first coach, the order was given to unhook the train coupling. As Tower reached in to close the air locks, Durrill misinterpreted what was happening and again slammed his pistol into Tower's ribs, screaming, "Make it snappy, you son of a bitch, or I'll blow your god damned heart out!"

As the air locks were closed and the uncoupling completed, Nash, who had remained in the engine, ordered engineer Miller to move the engine a distance equivalent to approximately three car lengths, thus separating the front and back halves. Nash and Miller departed the engine and joined Durrill and Tower between both sections of the train, where they were soon joined by express mail clerks Warren Burch and Charles Weiss. Nash ordered the four to set down on the tracks. At this point, Kelly, Curtis and Dixon appeared, firing their pistols into the air, and took their places standing guard over the rear section while Thayer and Spencer began rummaging through the mail cars in search of the Liberty Bonds. Nash, ever the calm and polite bandit, continually apologized to the four for Durrill's erratic behavior. As Durrill continually swore and waved his pistol about, Nash explained, "It's his first job and he let his nerves get the best of him." Nash also engaged the hostages in conversations that included the recent death of President Warren G. Harding and the merits of Samuel G. Blythe as a political writer.[15]

As the robbery was coming to a close, plans also called for the bandits to rob the passengers, but a quick-acting Pullman porter named T.J. Davis, who raced through the passenger cars locking doors, foiled any possibility of that. The seven bandits met between the two sections of train, where Nash took roll, accounting for all, and ordered them to the three getaway cars parked nearby.

In all, according to newspaper accounts, the robbery netted the bandits between $30,000 and $40,000 in bonds, cash and registered mail. Their plan had fallen apart as soon as it began. Charley Carson, who had departed the train, realized the engine had come to a stop soon after he departed and heard gunshots shortly thereafter. He was able to make his way to a phone box, where he notified railroad authorities. Within thirty minutes, Osage County sheriff C.A. Cook arrived at the scene. Within a few short hours, a large posse of local lawmen, as well as deputy U.S. marshal Alva McDonald, were on the case. By the first afternoon after the robbery, Ike Ogg had been arrested at his home. Within the next few days, every outlaw that could be found had been apprehended, questioned and subsequently released one by one. Earl Thayer was picked up in Oklahoma City by McDonald. The investigation progressed as Ogg began giving details and names to the authorities.

POST OFFICE DEPARTMENT

OFFICE OF THE INSPECTOR IN CHARGE CASE No. 56245-D

Kansas City, Mo., Sept. 4, 1923.

REWARD

The Post Office Department will pay a reward not exceeding Two Thousand Dollars ($2,000.00), for information leading to the arrest and conviction of each of the parties herein named and described.

Under paragraph "12" Postmaster General's "Notice of Reward," Order No. 7708:

> "When an offender is killed in the act of committing any of the crimes enumerated herein, OR IN RESISTING LAWFUL ARREST THEREFOR THE SAME REWARD MAY BE PAID AS THOUGH HE HAD BEEN TRIED AND CONVICTED."

These men are wanted for the hold-up and robbery of Missouri, Kansas & Texas Train 123 (PARSONS & OKLAHOMA RPO) near Okesa, Oklahoma, on the night of August 20, 1923.

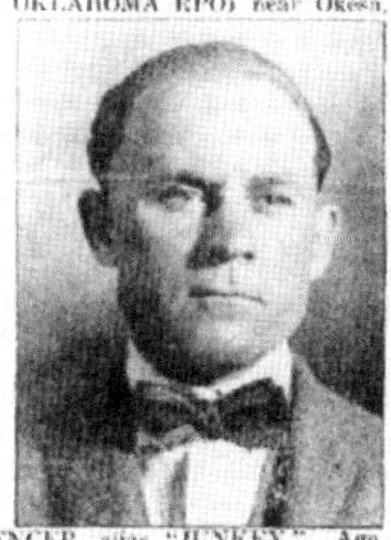

AL SPENCER, alias "JUNKEY." Age 36, eyes gray; hair chestnut; complexion medium; height 5 feet 6¼ inches; weight 135 to 140 pounds; build medium; athletic; teeth irregular.

FINGER PRINT CLASSIFICATION:
31 10 15
28 11 16

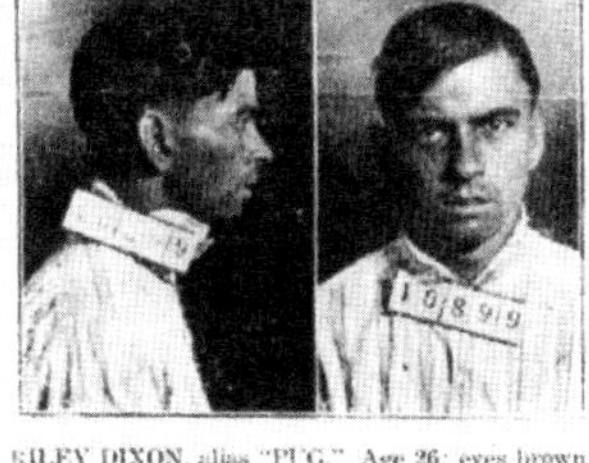

RILEY DIXON, alias "PUG." Age 26; eyes brown; hair dark chestnut; complexion medium; height 5 feet 5⅝ inches; weight 120 to 125; slender build. Has letters "R. D. D." tatooed in blue ink left forearm.

FINGER PRINT CLASSIFICATION:
32 — 1
24 — M

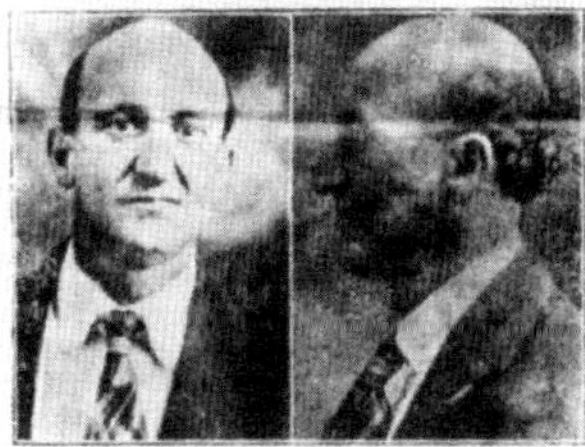

FRANK NASH: Age 33, eyes dark gray; hair very black, but bald on top head; height 5 feet 9¼ inches; weight 160 pounds; build medium slender; large Roman nose; coarse voice, but speaks good English; walks erect and fast. Has ½ inch scar over right eyebrow, also small scar over bridge of nose.

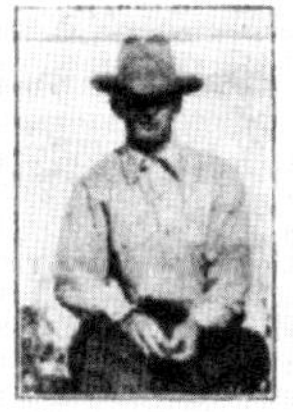

GROVER C. DURRILL: Age 35; eyes dark; hair dark, rather curly; complexion florid; height 5 feet 11 inches; weight 175 pounds.

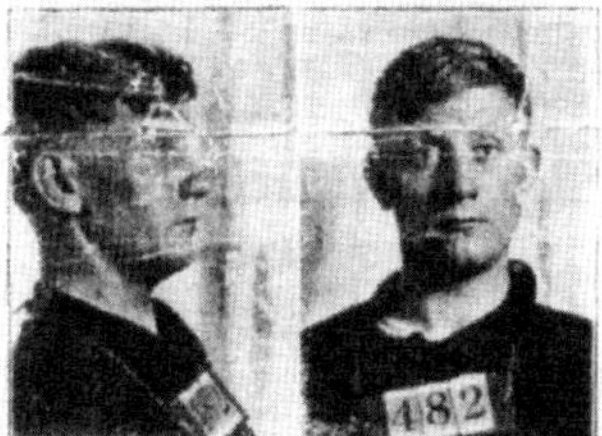

GEORGE [illegible], alias "WHITEY," etc. Age 28; height 5 feet 6¾ inches; weight 155 to 160 pounds. Medium build. Hair light chestnut; eyes blue; complexion fair. (The picture above was taken when this party was 22 years of age.)

FINGER PRINT CLASSIFICATION:
5 U 11 19
17 R 01 15

These men probably have in their possession the following described Liberty Bonds, stolen from the mails, and all banks and brokers are cautioned to keep a strict watch for any of the same.

Twenty one-thousand dollar Liberty Loan Coupon Bonds of the second issue, Serial numbers: D01324419; C01324418; A01081471; D00940734; E00025210; A00025211; B00025212; D00392039; D01335289; D00392094; D00026889; E00026890; A00026891; C00026893; D00026894; B00340667; C00340668; E00392015; A00392016; C00392028.

With the exception of DURRILL all of these men are ex-convicts; all are dangerous gun men and may be traveling together. They use high power automobiles, and when last seen were driving a Hudson Super-Six. This gang change automobiles frequently.

If these men are located, cause their immediate arrest, and notify the undersigned by telegraph, Government rate, collect.

L. A. JOHNSON,
Post Office Inspector in Charge,
Kansas City, Missouri

Post office "wanted" poster issued for the Al Spencer gang. *Courtesy of the author.*

Back to the subject of Al Spencer and his love of attention. A letter received on September 6 at the *Pawhuska Daily Capital* read:

> *You are clever Mr. McDonald and you also Mr. Adamson but don't think you are fooling me with all this bunk you have given out to the newspapers. I know what you're here for. I know you are after me. You may deny it to the newspapers from now till hell freezes over but I will be looking out for you and watching your movements just the same.*[16]

Spencer's bravado had apparently gotten the best of him before the robbery even took place. In his need to prove to the media that he was the outlaw he wished to be, he had told several people where and when the robbery was to take place. As the investigation unfolded, cigarette butt litter, trampled grass and other debris was found all along the area overlooking the scene of the crime. Apparently, the robbery had drawn quite a large number of curious onlookers. But unbeknownst to Spencer, the day the aforementioned letter was received, a wanted poster was released naming not only Spencer but also Riley Dixon, Frank Nash, Grover C. Durrill and George Fallon. By September 21, all had been arrested except Spencer and Nash. Spencer finally came to the end of the trail on September 15 near Caney, Kansas, when he was shot dead by a posse led by marshal

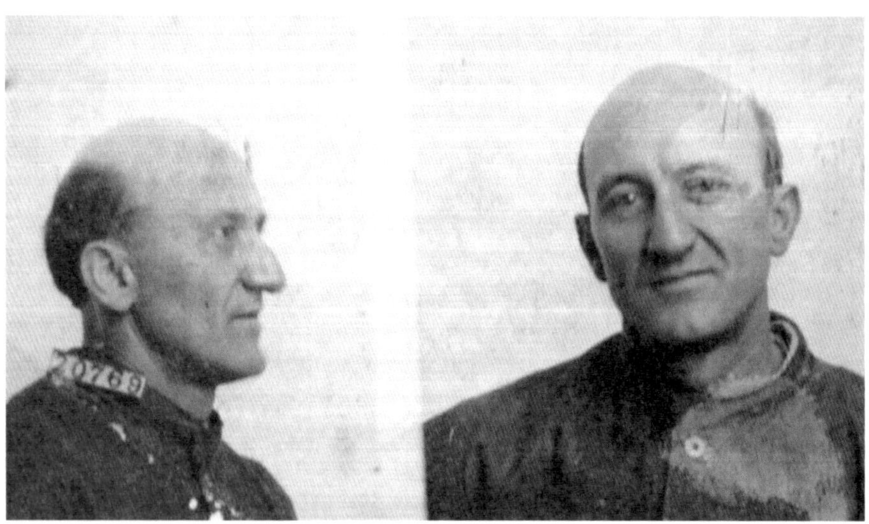

Oklahoma outlaw Frank Nash's USP Leavenworth mug shot. *Courtesy National Archives and Records Administration.*

Alva McDonald.[17] Nash, who had fled to Mexico, married a local woman in an attempt to produce an alibi. After being spotted by an informant, Nash was coaxed back across the Rio Grande during an attempted cattle-rustling scheme in which he was arrested by McDonald on November 9. On March 1, 1924, at the federal courthouse in Oklahoma City, all who had taken part in what would be the last armed train robbery in Oklahoma history were sentenced to 25 years and sent to Leavenworth.[18]

4

RANGER

Thomas Bruce "Tom" White was appointed warden of the Big L on March 7, 1927, one day after his 46th birthday. White had served a stint as the institution's deputy warden and interim warden prior to the appointment. This would mark the first time in the institution's history that a man with a career in law enforcement would be appointed to its highest post.

To the average person, White's career officially began with his enlistment in Company A of the Texas Rangers under the command of Captain J.A. Brooks on September 18, 1906. But to understand the man White would become, one only has to look back upon his upbringing in a one-room log cabin in rural Oak Hill, Texas, about five miles from the city of Austin.[19] He was the third of five children—four boys and one girl.

As the family grew, Tom White's father, Robert Emmet, and mother, Maggie, expanded their home. Working alongside the family were a couple of first-generation freed slaves named Anthony Solomon and Meedie. The devotion to the family—a loyalty and devotion that would carry them all through the toughest of hardship—was equally reciprocated. Maggie passed away when Tom was six years old, and it was Meedie who stepped up and took care of the kids as well as preparing meals and keeping house. Joining the family shortly thereafter was Tom's widowed aunt Lina.

As Tom neared the age of eight, his father was elected to the position of Travis County sheriff. The family's new home was so close to the jail that Tom and the rest of his siblings could look right into the cell area from their bedroom window. It was also from this window where Tom witnessed firsthand the principles that governed his father's actions as sheriff and how he treated all with whom he came in contact. These principles would guide Tom throughout his career and the remainder of his life.

The first and most important principle was to never consider a person's color or station in life in any dealings you have with them. The poor and underprivileged should always receive the same consideration as the more fortunate. Second, never ask another person to do anything you yourself would not do. This principle was the rule of conduct that led the sheriff to perform his own hangings. Executions were also viewed from the window up above—the same bedroom window from which Tom and his siblings witnessed them firsthand as well.

All four of the White boys would follow in their father's footsteps. The eldest, John Dudley, joined the Texas Rangers in 1905 and served until 1911, then served for a brief time as a Houston city police officer and a U.S. mounted customs agent before reenlisting with the Rangers in 1916. On July 12, 1918, John Dudley, along with fellow Ranger Walter Rowe, was attempting to arrest two brothers who had deserted from the army. Both Rangers were ambushed, and Rowe was shot in the hip while John Dudley White was fatally shot from behind. The second-oldest, Coleman (Coley), was elected to the position his father had held, Travis County sheriff. James, the youngest son, known by his nickname of "Doc," served as a Houston city police officer, Texas Ranger, customs agent, Prohibition agent and FBI agent. As an FBI agent, Doc was involved with bringing down John Dillinger and his gang, the apprehension of Machine Gun Kelly and the gun battle that brought an end to Ma Barker and members of her gang.[20]

Tom White's career in law enforcement spanned a total of fifty years. After serving as a Texas Ranger from 1906 until 1909, he then served until 1917 as a special agent first for the Santa Fe Railroad and second for the Southern Pacific. In 1917, Tom became a special agent for the FBI and served until 1927.

Tom's earliest assignments as a Ranger included breaking up cattle rustling and bootlegging operations. On one such operation, the young Ranger White accompanied Captain Brooks and Sergeant Dunnaway to Kent County to break up a group of cattle rustlers. Upon entering the town of Clairemont, Captain Brooks tended to business while Dunnaway and White ventured into the general store for provisions. As they stepped inside, the sergeant asked the young Ranger where his Winchester was. Tom's reply of "in my saddle scabbard out front" was met with a stern lecture about survival and the order, "You don't ever do that! Always take your guns with

A. G. O. FORM 21.
Authorized July 7, 1905.

665-705-2h

ENLISTMENT, OATH OF SERVICE, AND DESCRIPTION RANGER FORCE.

Company A Ranger Force, Station Colorado City,

THE STATE OF TEXAS,
COUNTY OF Travis

I, Thomas B. White, born in March 6th, 1881, in the State of Texas, aged 25 years and 6 months, and by occupation a Ranchman *do hereby acknowledge to have voluntarily enlisted this day of* 18th Sept., 1906, as a private in the Ranger Force of this State, for the period of two years, unless sooner discharged by proper authority. And I do also agree to accept from the State of Texas such bounty, pay, subsistence and other expenses as are or may be established by law. And I do solemnly swear that I will faithfully and impartially discharge and perform all the duties incumbent on me as an officer of the Ranger Force according to the best of my skill and ability, agreeably to the Constitution and laws of the United States and of this State, and I do further solemnly swear that since the adoption of the Constitution of this State, I being a citizen of this State, have not fought a duel with deadly weapons, nor have I acted as second in carrying a challenge, or aided, advised or assisted any person thus offending. And I furthermore swear that I have not, directly nor indirectly, paid, offered or promised to pay, contributed nor promised to contribute, any money or valuable thing, or promised any public office or employment, to secure my appointment. So help me God.

Thomas B White

Subscribed and sworn to before me this 18th day of September A. D. 1906,

E.M. Phelps
Notary Public Travis Co.
Texas.

Thomas Bruce White's law enforcement career officially began with his enlistment in the Texas Rangers on September 18, 1906. *Courtesy Texas Ranger Hall of Fame and Museum.*

you. It don't make no difference where you go, you always keep your guns right with you. Go get your Winchester right now and bring it in here and keep it with you at all times!"

On October 17, 1909, Tom White married Bessie Patterson in Weatherford. The work of a Texas Ranger always kept them on the move, and his monthly take-home pay of $40 was hardly suitable for a young married couple. These, along with the loss of his good friend and frequent partner, Ranger N.P. "Doc" Thomas, provided ample reasons for White to leave the Texas Rangers. White and Thomas had accompanied Company A to Amarillo to shut down several bootlegging operations. Many of the town's most reputable people were connected to the bootleggers and were enraged by the Rangers' interference and arrests. Most of the Rangers had withdrawn from Amarillo, but Thomas remained. At 10:00 a.m. on January 5, 1909, Thomas was sitting in the office of the county attorney. Deputy sheriff Jim Keeton entered the room while the attorney was in another office, and after a brief exchange, Keeton drew his pistol and shot Thomas in the head. On October 18, 1909, Tom White reported in Amarillo to work for the Santa Fe Railroad.

From then until 1917, White had gone from tracking and capturing cattle rustlers, thieves and murderers to investigating multitudes of lawsuits brought against his employers. His general attitude toward these individuals was far less tolerant than the one he had for those he had brought to justice for violent crimes. The violent offender had a certain honesty about themselves and what they were. White often commented, "I'd rather see a man take money from his victim at the point of a gun than to use lies and trickery." The instances of fraudulent claims of severe injuries that led to disability, loss of property and claims of mistreatment coupled with sabotage to railroad property and labor disputes taught valuable lessons to the investigator. He learned a considerable amount about the behavior and conduct of people in regard to the law. Along the way, he gained a vast knowledge of investigative techniques and how the smallest little detail that could be easily overlooked or ignored could turn out to be the vital point in solving the case.

The biggest break in White's career came on the heels of his biggest disappointment. White had volunteered for military service in the early stages of World War I and was unable to pass the entrance physical due to a medical procedure. Shortly thereafter, an offer to join the FBI presented itself. The era leading up to the war had seen a steady increase in interstate travel by people all over the country and the transportation of goods across state lines. Criminal elements were also breaching state boundaries and extending enterprises. This new wave of criminal enterprise caused considerable jurisdictional issues for local and state authorities. Congress, recognizing these problems, began to create more federal laws, thus extending the authority of federal law enforcement agencies. The Dyer Act prohibiting the transportation of stolen automobiles across state lines and the Mann Act (aka the White-Slave Traffic Act) were two such laws.

White's early days with the FBI saw him on cases involving the illegal sale of weapons and ammunition to Mexican revolutionaries along the Texas-Mexico border. During these early years, the White family moved to Houston, where Tom was placed in charge of that city's field office. His new

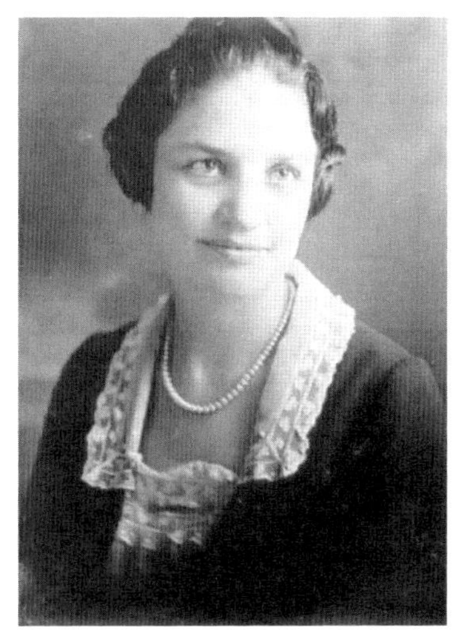

Mabel Walker Willebrandt. *Courtesy Library of Congress.*

title became inspector, and his job was to inspect FBI offices in Atlanta, Georgia; St. Paul, Minnesota; and Portland, Oregon.

In 1920, the Volstead Act took effect; it prohibited the importation and sale of intoxicating spirits, giving rise to bootleggers and gangsters. In 1921, President Warren G. Harding appointed thirty-two-year-old Mabel Walker Willebrandt to the position of assistant attorney general. Willebrandt had made a name for herself as the first female public defender of Los Angeles County. Her duties were to oversee the prosecution of the Volstead violators, income tax litigation and the Federal Prison Service. The largest hurdle facing Willebrandt was the widespread corruption of law enforcement officers and federal and state officials. Bootlegging began raking in millions, and it was easy to pay officials to look the other way.

One of the first cases Willebrandt assigned to White was the infiltration of agents into a group known as the Big Four, a bootlegging operation run by Willie Haar. The operation involved a fleet of boats bringing in liquor from Cuba, the Bahamas and other parts of the Caribbean. Once the boats landed, the liquor was transported all over the southeastern United States by truck. Working on a tip, White and a group of undercover agents entered a warehouse and located $70,000 and records used in the operation. Haar, his three associates and sixty-four other members of the operation were convicted and sentenced to federal prison. With the records in hand, it was found that Haar himself owed more than $1 million in back taxes.

One of the biggest cases of corruption involving a FBI agent was the case of Franklin Dodge Jr. Dodge was the son of a prominent attorney, businessman and state representative from Lansing, Michigan. Dodge was one of the agents who had worked alongside Tom White on the Willie Haar case. Dodge had been sent undercover into the federal prison at Atlanta, Georgia, posing as an inmate to look into the corruption of prison officials, including Warden Albert Sartain. During the investigation, he met Cincinnati multimillionaire bootlegger George Remus and struck up a friendship. With his cover blown, Dodge was taken out of the prison, and he soon resigned his position with the FBI and commenced an affair with

Remus' wife, Imogene, who had power of attorney over her husband's vast empire. The pair tried to have Remus deported and even paid a hitman $15,000, but both attempts failed. Dodge even convinced Imogene to begin liquidating her husband's assets, including selling his Fleischmann Distillery and hiding as much money as possible. In 1927, shortly after his release, Remus shot Imogene to death in a park in Cincinnati in broad daylight. Representing himself, Remus portrayed himself as the victim and Dodge and Imogene as the villains. He was acquitted of murder by reason of temporary insanity.

As the Dodge debacle was unfolding, Tom White had returned to his duties and his family in Houston. While on a routine inspection of the New Mexico field office, he received orders to immediately report to the FBI director's office. Upon his arrival at J. Edgar Hoover's office, they made their way to the attorney general's office for a meeting with attorney general Harlan Stone and assistant attorney general Mabel Willebrandt. A plan was put forth for Atlanta warden Albert Sartain to report to the attorney general's office and for White to report to the Atlanta prison as acting warden. It was also decided that Colonel W.J. (Wild Bill) Donovan would assist in the investigation, and the army post near Atlanta would render military assistance if needed.

Upon their arrival on October 1, 1924, the investigators were besieged with requests to speak with them by nearly the entire inmate population, which totaled 2,500. Accusations of mistreatment, favoritism, bribery and corruption of all types began to overwhelm White and Donovan. It was also apparent that inmates, staff and officials were keeping an eye on everything that developed. Those under investigation were amongst the most popular in the community, and intimidation and threats were cast upon White's family. Tom decided it was best for them to return to Houston until the investigation was resolved.

Through interviews with inmates and staff, it was discovered that many of the influential inmates had been paying prison officials for preferential treatment, easy job assignments and special living arrangements. Payments ranged from $15 to $5,000. It was also discovered that a $50-per-card poker game was a regular activity above the garage at the warden's residence. In one of the most shocking developments, prison chaplain Thomas P. Hayden was found to be on the take. Once placed on the hot seat, Hayden admitted to accepting a bribe and implicated the others. He admitted that shortly after the arrest of Willie Haar, he had accompanied a close friend of Warden Sartain named Laurence Riehl to Savannah, where they received

$10,500 after they assured the bootleggers that they would receive special treatment once they arrived. Millionaire bootleggers George Remus and Emmanuel Kessler both admitted to paying between $2,000 and $5,000 for special food, special sleeping quarters and preferred treatment. Two other bootleggers even paid $2,500 for the privilege of having their meals served in the chaplain's quarters. Broadway producer, director, songwriter and composer Earl Carroll had been tried for perjury and sentenced to a year and a day. Instead of arriving at the prison in handcuffs, he arrived via a private berth of a train, and upon his arrival was quartered in an apartment above the warden's garage. It was also discovered that one of Carroll's actresses frequently visited him at the apartment and was entertaining the warden as well.

Other allegations began to surface about high-powered inmates being allowed to keep suites at a local hotel, where they threw wild parties at which women and large stocks of expensive liquor were commonplace. One inmate named Ben Hance confided that of the several suspicious escapes that had occurred prior to White's arrival, one involved the notorious criminal Gerald Chapman. Chapman had spent most of his adult life in prison for bank robbery, armed robberies, bootlegging and mail truck robberies. His reputation of being polite as well as sporting a British accent during his exploits earned him the name "the Gentleman Bandit." Hance was able to provide the whereabouts of Chapman, which allowed authorities to apprehend him in Muncie, Indiana, in January 1925.

Upon completion of his investigation, White turned over his findings to J. Edgar Hoover, who presented them to the attorney general. On January 28, 1925, a grand jury returned an indictment charging Warden Albert E. Sartain, Deputy Warden Looney J. Fletcher and Laurence Riehl with receiving bribes from seven different inmates in order for those inmates to receive special treatment. Their trial began on February 9 and concluded with sentencing on February 20, 1925. Deputy Warden Fletcher was acquitted of all charges. Riehl was found guilty and was sentenced to one year and one day. Warden Sartain was found guilty and sentenced to eighteen months in the very penitentiary of which he was once in charge.[21] For his cooperation in the investigation, chaplain Thomas P. Hayden was not named or charged in the original indictment.

Following the convictions in the aforementioned case, Tom White returned to Houston, where his next year was relatively quiet. He was able to spend more time with his wife and two sons. His job of inspecting field offices, along with the occasional breakup of bootlegging operations, interstate transfer of stolen automobiles and general racketeering aided in the rather unspectacular year. Once again, a call from the office of J. Edgar Hoover requesting Tom's presence in Washington only meant one thing: break time was over.

In 1906, the Osage tribe in Oklahoma occupied approximately 657 acres of land in Osage County. Their total head count was 2,229 members on said land. With the discovery of oil that same year, along with money held in trust by the United States government, the Osage tribe had become the richest group of people in the world. By 1923, there were an estimated total of 8,579 wells operating within the boundaries of the Osage reservation, producing an estimated $12,000 for every man, woman and child, with the average family of five raking in $60,000 per year.[22] It didn't take long before this piqued the interest of local white swindlers. In short order, it became common to see grand pianos in virtually every yard and entire families being hauled about in limousines mainly consisting of horse-drawn funeral hearses. Another practice commonly employed was to marry a member of the tribe. Unfortunately, those marriages didn't last long, because as fate would have it, the Osage member of the family would suddenly die, leaving their spouse as the sole inheritor of their oil shares. The principal culprits in the deaths were a rash of mysterious suicides and freak accidents. By the time the Osage discovered this angle was being employed and stopped marrying, single Native Americans began meeting the same fate. Again, suicide and accidental deaths were to blame.

This is where local cattleman William "Bill" Hale stepped up and thrived. Hale used bribery, intimidation and extortion in order to gain control of the oil rights of the newly deceased. Hale's nephews Bryan and Ernest Burkhart were two of his associates who carried out the murders. Ernest had even gone as far as marrying a native Osage girl named Mollie Kyle, the youngest daughter of Jimmie and Lizzie Que. With Jimmie inheriting the head rights of his first wife, his and Lizzie's head rights and the shares of their four daughters, the Kyle family was one of the wealthiest of the Osage Nation. Upon Jimmie's death, the remaining members of the family—Lizzie Que, Minnie, Rita, Anna and Mollie—became the sole heirs of a vast and expanding fortune.

Minnie, the eldest daughter, married a man named William Smith and died soon after; after a brief grieving period, the young Smith married Minnie's sister Rita. Shortly thereafter, sister Anna was murdered, and their mother Lizzie Que died. This left Rita and Mollie as the sole beneficiaries sharing their wealth with their respective husbands, Burkhart and Smith.

The differences between the two brothers-in-law were as clear as night and day. Smith never truly trusted Burkhart, knowing of his relationship with Bill Hale. Smith also claimed that Hale owed him a sum of $6,000, which Hale had refused to pay. This left Burkhart and Hale with a determination that would only favor them.

Piecing together this investigation was most difficult given the time frame of several years along with unreliable witnesses, witnesses who could not be located, those who refused to talk for fear of retribution and the vast list of those who were already dead. Every angle of this case was worked, and an enormous number of undercover agents were involved.[23] Tom White had decided that returning to his Texas Ranger ways would be quite useful in selecting the agents he needed. He found agents who could pose as oil field workers, cowboys, insurance salesmen, hoboes, drifters and an Indian medicine man. The men he used were also well accustomed to the customs, habits and beliefs of the Osage.

During the investigation, it had been discovered that Anna had received a call on May 21, 1921, and advised that her mother, Lizzie Que, had become very ill and was at Anna's sister Mollie's house. It is reported that during the day, Anna had been drinking moonshine, and sometime after dinner, she had left Mollie's house with Ernest and Bryan Burkhart. Anna was solely infatuated with Bryan, thus she trusted him. It was reported that the trio had met up with Kelsey Morrison and possibly his wife and had stopped by the home of Bill Hale, where Bryan was given a .32-caliber pistol. After leaving, the five spent the remaining hours of that night and into the next morning barhopping. It was determined that Ernest left with Morrison's wife, leaving Bryan, Kelsey and Anna to make their way back to Mollie's house. On the way, the car in which they were riding pulled off the road next to a wooded area. Bryan and Kelsey pulled the drunken Anna from the car; Bryan held her up, and Kelsey shot her through the head. Anna's body was discovered five days later with her back against a cliff, the pistol near her left hand and a soda bottle full of whiskey in her right.

It was also discovered that even though it took a few years, the time had come for the vast Kyle fortune to finally land in the hands of Mollie and her husband, Ernest. On March 23, 1923, while Rita and William Smith slept, a large explosion occurred that completely demolished their home and killed Rita and William. The cause was determined to be a keg of nitroglycerin that had been detonated in the couple's garage, located directly below their bedroom. The force of the explosion was so great that it had torn through six inches of concrete flooring, creating a crater six feet in diameter and three feet deep. The killers had even poured kerosene around the house, causing everything to be destroyed by fire. The detonator was found a block from the explosion. Also killed was a young white girl who had been working for the Smiths as a maid.

Evidence in the death of the Smiths showed that Hale and Burkhart had tried to contract out the killing of the Smiths as early as 1920 but had been repeatedly turned down. In early 1923, Ernest and a friend named John Ramsey travelled to Ripley, Oklahoma, where they met with a man named Asa "Ace" Kirby, who gladly accepted the job for a payment of $2,000. After the job was complete, Hale told Kirby about a general store that often had large amounts of cash, diamonds and jewelry on hand due in large part to the store's owner living on the property. On the night of the robbery, Kirby entered the store that he had staked out the previous afternoon. Shortly afterward, Kirby's life of crime was ended by a full charge of buckshot from the owner's shotgun. Seems the store owner had been tipped off about the robbery by his good friend Bill Hale.

Another business associate of Hale, Henry Roan Horse, was to meet a similar fate. It appears that Roan Horse had a weakness for whiskey, which Hale was all too willing to provide in return for the Indian's property, which mainly consisted of cattle and grazing land. Hale had even purchased a $25,000 life-insurance policy for Roan Horse but had increasingly become concerned that Roan Horse would die or commit suicide before the policy was in effect for one year. After Hale confided in his good friend Henry Grammar, a plan was hatched. Grammar advised Hale that a bootlegger named John Ramsey was willing to do anything for a price. For $500 and a new Ford roadster, the plan was put to Ramsey. Ramsey watched Roan Horse and decided to sit next to him at a restaurant counter, where Ramsey assured Roan Horse that he could get him the best-quality liquor at an affordable price. Ramsey and Roan Horse had several meetings afterward during which liquor was exchanged for cash. On February 6, 1923, Roan Horse and Ramsey met at the usual spot at the usual time and sat slamming back drinks on the running boards of their cars. When Roan Horse decided it was time to leave, Ramsey allowed him to get behind the wheel of the car and then followed along behind. For the next few minutes, as Roan Horse sat in the car and Ramsey stood at the window, the two men continued their conversation. After exchanging goodbyes, Ramsey raised a .45-caliber pistol and sent a bullet through Roan Horse's head; the bullet entered behind the left ear. Hale served as a pallbearer for his "friend's" funeral.

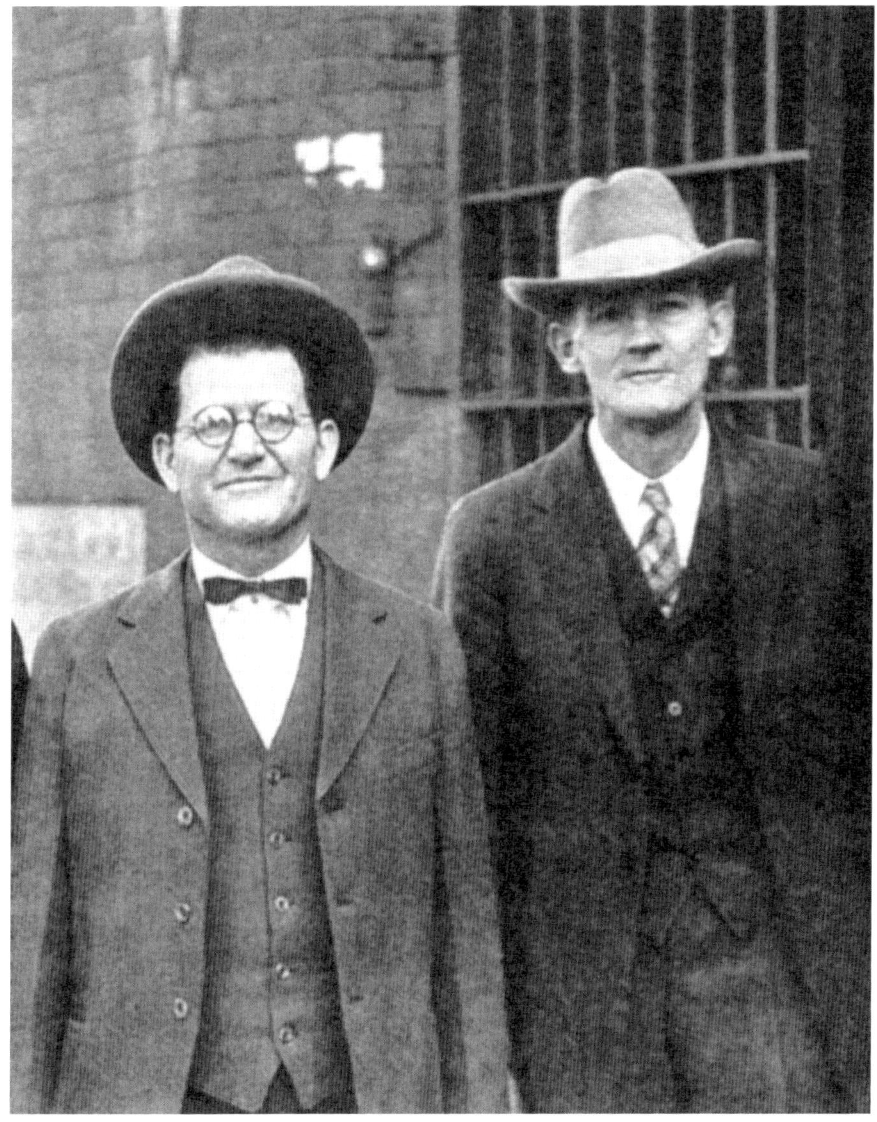

William K. Hale (*left*) and John Ramsey on their way to Leavenworth. *Courtesy of the author.*

William K. Hale and John Ramsey were taken into custody in January 1926; in April, Kelsey Morrison and Bryan Burkhart were arrested. During the interrogation process, Ernest Burkhart struck a plea deal. In exchange for a life sentence at the Oklahoma State Penitentiary, he turned state's evidence against his uncle and Ramsey. Ramsey, in turn, provided prosecutors with details of how Hale had hired him to commit the murder of Henry Roan Horse. He also confessed to the killings of William and Rita Smith and their housekeeper, Nettie Brookshire, implicating Hale as the mastermind of that plot as well. Also implicated by Ramsey was Henry Grammar, who mysteriously died shortly after the Smiths. Morrison admitted to the murder of Anna Brown and also implicated Hale. He also received a life sentence to be served in McAlester. Bryan Burkhart provided the prosecution with evidence and was not tried. After several mistrials, deadlocked juries and appeals, Hale was sentenced to life imprisonment in January 1929 and Ramsey was sentenced to life imprisonment in November that same year. Both were to serve in the federal prison at Leavenworth. Upon entering the prison, they were greeted by Warden Thomas B. White.

5

OVERCROWDING, CONSPIRACIES, DISSENSION AND THREE BISCUITS BILL

By the end of World War I, USP Leavenworth was entering its final decade of construction. The population of the institution had remained steady, with a low of 1,200 and a high of 2,000 inmates on average. With each passing year, more federal criminal laws were passed by Congress. Laws such as the Espionage and Sedition Act, Dyer Act, Volstead Act, Esch-Cummins Transportation Act and the Emergency Quota and Immigration Act, combined with the looming unemployment rate brought on by the Great Depression, sent prison populations spiraling out of control. Leavenworth was no exception.

The design of these laws was intended to lead to improving the everyday American's way of life. It had quite the opposite effect. The Roaring Twenties saw a significant rise in crime across the board.[24] The murder rate, for example, rose from 6,800 in 1920 to 8,400 or more yearly through 1929. Thirty cities across the United States reported a 24 percent increase in all crimes between 1920 and 1921 alone. Before the passage of Prohibition, there were a total of 4,000 federal prisoners, with fewer than 3,000 housed in federal prisons. By 1932, the number of federal prisoners had risen by 561 percent with the federal prison population rising 361 percent. Leavenworth's capacity was rated at 1,500 inmates, but by the mid-1920s, the institution was consistently housing approximately 4,500 inmates throughout most of the decade.

With each passing day, scores of new inmates arrived, placing more burdens upon the institution to provide basics such as food, clothing and a place to sleep. The institution became more violent. With the ever-growing inmate population, programs were designed to occupy their time. Prison industries, such as the broom and shoe factory, began instituting additional shifts. Feeding the population became an all-day affair. As one meal shift was ending, another was beginning. All over the institution, inmates were allowed to keep pets such as dogs, cats, fish and birds. Fish tanks and bird cages were common fixtures amongst the population and found in offices and cells all over the institution. Institution beautification programs were started, pitting cell houses and work assignments against each other for the right to go first to chow, the movies or the recreation yard. Large sprawling gardens and ornate landscapes were located throughout the institution. The institution's baseball teams practiced for hours on the small field located behind the shops area.

Finding solutions to the overcrowding issue was the task of Warden W.I. Biddle. Biddle had come to Leavenworth with his parents when he was thirteen. After finding work as an apprentice in the machine molding trade, he found himself laid off during a particularly cold winter. He soon found work as a reporter for the *Leavenworth Times* under editor Colonel Daniel Reid Anthony. Although he found Biddle's reporting skills suspect, Anthony admired the young man's work ethic. He put Biddle to work as a recorder for the Leavenworth County Republican Committee. He also served as the register clerk and postmaster of the local post office. Serving as the campaign manager for U.S. Representative D.R. Anthony Jr. landed him an appointment on the board of directors of the Kansas State Penitentiary, where he oversaw the business affairs of the institution as well as discipline and parole. Biddle was instrumental in reforming discipline at the institution by doing away with stripes, the water cure and the frame crib as forms of discipline. Also abolished was the convict labor system that hired inmates out to local factories. He established a brick plant, twine plant and ice plant and acquired funding for a new, more modern dining facility. In 1921, Biddle used his friendship with Anthony, who was then serving his seventh term as a representative, to gain his appointment to be Leavenworth's warden by newly elected President Warren G. Harding.[25]

Unafraid to use his connections, Biddle considered himself a visionary. He was able to seek and be granted permission to hire more officers. A new, more modern prison industries building was constructed, and even before completion, plans had already been implemented for the expansion of that facility. The brick factory that had been established in the early years of construction was now beginning to churn outs its last bricks. Those not

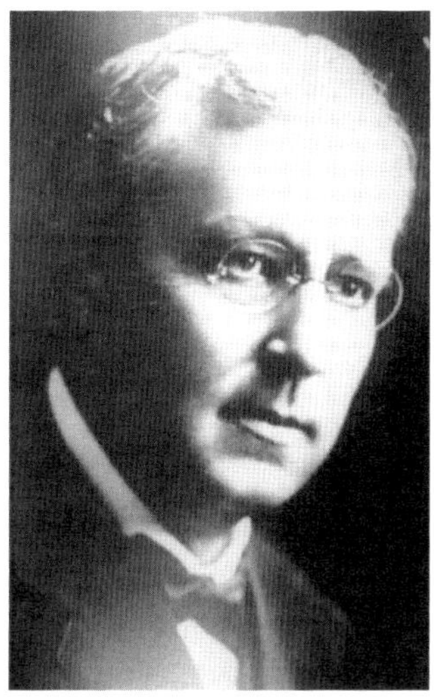

For unknown reasons, many inmates referred to Warden W.I. Biddle as "Three Biscuits Bill." Biddle had parlayed his political favors into his position as warden of Leavenworth. *Courtesy of the author.*

used in the final stages of construction were used to pave the new entryway to the nearby Fort Leavenworth and Grant Avenue. In appreciation for all the work the Sisters of Charity had done, the inmates were allowed to use some of the brick to pave the entryway and main drive at nearby Saint Mary College. The last of the brick was used to repair the nearby Fort Leavenworth Bridge, a combination railroad and traffic bridge that had been abandoned due to unsafe conditions caused by several fires. Upon completion, the bridge was once again a vital link between Kansas and Missouri. Biddle, along with his friend D.R. Anthony Jr., was able to secure ownership of the 1,900 acres located on the Missouri side of the river from the War Department. Once cleared, plans called for the construction of farm dormitories where trustys, short-timers and those who had served most of their long sentences could live and work, thus relieving—at least for the moment—the overcrowding at the main institution.

As younger officers were hired, a disparity began to rise between them and the older, more experienced officers. Many of those who had been around since the early days resented the fact that the officers now being hired were making the same pay. At that time, an officer's yearly salary was $1,500. It didn't matter whether you were there thirty years or thirty minutes. Many times, when the younger officers asked questions of the more experienced, they were usually met with, "get up there on those galleries and learn how I did!" Issues also existed between the officers and civilian employees who worked in the shops, factories and other work details. Each of the different jobsites had an officer assigned to them to supervise the inmates. The officers were responsible for issuing passes, maintaining inmate accountability and keeping the peace. There were many instances in which two inmates would get into an altercation, the officer would jump in to break it up and the civilian employee would just stand by and watch. After all, it wasn't their job to police the inmate population. Inmates were also responsible for alerting officers of institutional emergencies. As overcrowding became worse, institutional emergencies became an everyday occurrence. A steep increase in fights (with and without weapons) and murders was reported. An increase in inmate suicides was also noted.

During the World War I era and into the early 1920s, work was beginning on the administration building and front stairs of the main institution. One of the largest groups to see the inside of Leavenworth at that time was the International Workers of the World (IWW) labor union. Over 100 members received ten- to twenty-year sentences for speaking out against involvement in the war. Many were tried on charges of seditious conspiracy, injuring civil rights, obstruction of military service and espionage. During the early stages of their incarceration, a series of arson fires took place. Many of these fires were small and did little damage, but two caused major damage. The back section of A cell house was near completion when scaffolding was set ablaze. The fire became so intense that it warped the steel bars on the cell fronts and cracked the cement and other masonry. The locking system was a total loss. This set back the opening of that section of cells another five years. The fires created the additional duty of fire watch for officers assigned to areas around the institution. On one such evening, one of the fire watch officers checking the shop areas shortly after the 4:00 p.m. count discovered that one wall of the broom factory was totally engulfed in flames. The building suffered major structural damage to that area, and once the fire was put out, it was discovered that the area had been doused with gasoline.

Of those incarcerated under the Espionage Act, one inmate arrived who would stir the air of conspiracy for years to come. Ricardo Flores Magón had initially been received at McNeil Island, Washington, after receiving a twenty-year sentence for obstruction of military service, violation of the Trading with the Enemy Act, mailing non-mailable matter and conspiracy. He was received at Leavenworth on November 3, 1919. A self-proclaimed Mexican anarchist, Flores Magón had aligned himself with the IWW. In March 1918, he had published a manifesto to the Anarchists and Workers of the World suggesting that the demise of the "old society" was at hand and encouraging everyone to fan the flames of discontent that had been lit by tyranny. Many Flores Magón sympathizers had written letters to the president and attorney general, and even Warden Biddle had responded to claims that the inmate was receiving less than adequate medical attention. At the time, Flores Magón was writing to his supporters and telling them of his diminished eyesight, trouble walking and deteriorating health. Letters from other members of the IWW also claimed he was in deteriorating health. In his report to Washington, Biddle wrote, "He [Flores Magón] is

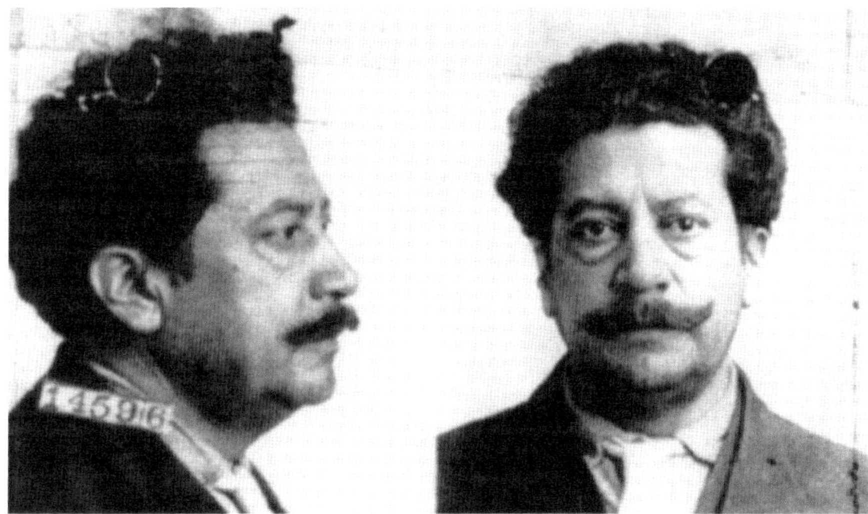

Ricardo Flores Magón. *Courtesy National Archives and Records Administration.*

a well-educated cunning Mexican trying to stir things up." Flores Magón passed away on November 11, 1922, and in his official report to the warden, Dr. A.F. Yohe wrote,

> *The night attendant at the hospital was called by [the] guard in Cell House "B" about 4:15 o'clock this morning. The attendant went over promptly and found Flores Magón suffering with distress and pain about the heart, he examined him and returned to the hospital for medicine. While the attendant was returning to the hospital the guard called again and stated that Flores Magón was dead. The body was immediately brought over to the hospital and examined by me this morning. It is my opinion that Flores Magón died of angina pectoris. You will, no doubt, recall that Flores Magón had been recently examined by both doctors Langworthy and myself and in those examinations we were unable to find any evidence of disease of heart* [sic]. *Prompt service was rendered Flores Magón and he was not neglected in any way.*[26]

Many of the institution's inmates, especially those who had formed an allegiance with Flores Magón, were becoming restless and irritated over conditions they perceived as mistreatment. Widespread rumors ran rampant throughout the institution that officers had actually murdered the inmate by strangulation. All of this came to a boiling point just three days later.

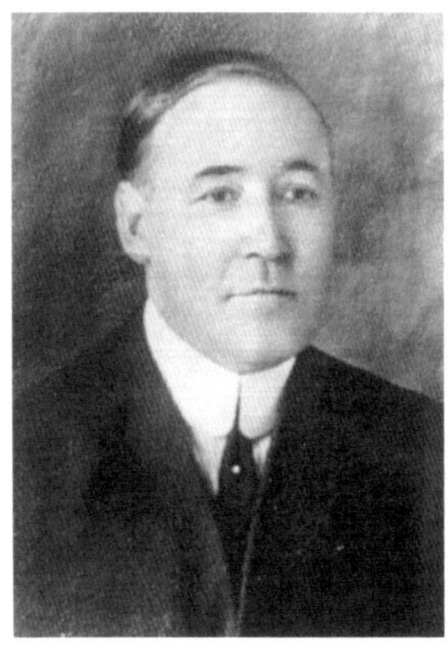

Andrew H. Leonard served 26 years at the prison. It was during the 1901 escape that Leonard injured his knee and was almost killed. Inmates had nicknamed him Captain "Bull" Leonard, and his brother-in-law Martin Lingual was nicknamed the "big Swede." *Courtesy Leavenworth Public Library.*

On November 14, inmate Joe Martinez was assigned to the coal-shoveling detail in the institution's powerhouse when an officer approached to escort him to B cell house for a haircut. Upon arrival at the cell house, Martinez had failed to remove his cap and was instructed to do so by another officer. The inmate barber instructed Martinez to clean the coal dust from his face; refusing, Martinez turned and walked out of the barbershop. Suddenly, the inmate barber saw Martinez produce a weapon and alerted the officers to look out. A total of six officers confronted the armed inmate and ordered him to submit to a pat search. As one of the officers attempted to search him, Martinez lunged forward, stabbing the officer in the shoulder. As the other officers attempted to subdue the inmate, they, too, were stabbed.

Captain Andrew H. Leonard was on his way to the east gate to release the outside work details when an inmate alerted him of the emergency. As Leonard was responding, he was joined by Officer Martin Lingual, and they began an immediate search of the grounds for the assailant. As they approached the front of the powerhouse, they were confronted by the weapon-wielding inmate. As they attempted to subdue Martinez, he broke free, running toward the top of a large coal pile. Hampered by the leg he had broken years before during the mutiny of November 1901, Leonard gave chase. As he reached the top of the pile of coal, he stumbled and fell forward. Martinez delivered a crushing blow to the captain's chest. As he sunk slowly to his knees, Leonard exclaimed, "He got me!"[27]

As the captain lay dying, Officer Lingual lunged forward; Martinez, now slashing the weapon back and forth, disemboweled the officer and sent him crashing to the ground. Arriving on scene armed with pistols were Officer E.N. Smith and Deputy Warden Fred G. Zerbst. Inmate Martinez attempted to climb upon a coal car and was shot twice by Smith—once in the knee and once in the stomach. After falling to the ground, the inmate crawled his way into the coal bunker located just inside the door of the powerhouse. As other Mexican inmates drew the attention of Martinez, two Negro inmates entered the bunker, subduing the killer.[28]

As the family of Martin Lingual made their way to his bedside at the institution, they found the officer—stitched from one side of his stomach to the other—sitting up in bed smoking a cigarette. When he was told that his longtime friend had died, he reportedly broke down and cried. In 2002, I met with Leonard's only surviving daughter, Mercedes. She related that on the morning of her father's death, he had made their mother breakfast in bed and then uncharacteristically went from room to room kissing each of his two daughters and infant son, telling them "I love you," then went to work. Two hours later, he was dead. She also relayed that when Deputy Warden Zerbst went to the warden's office to advise Warden Biddle that Leonard had died, "they found that coward hiding behind his drapes in fear the inmates were coming after him." Captain Leonard lay in state at the family home until his Mass of Christian Burial was conducted at the Old Immaculate Conception Cathedral. A funeral procession led by officers included dignitaries from the Department of Justice and four inmates from the institution. Captain Andrew H. Leonard was laid to rest at the Leavenworth National Cemetery at Fort Leavenworth.

By the mid-1920s, assistant attorney general Mabel Walker Willebrandt and other ranking officials of the Federal Prison Service had become weary of Warden Biddle over allegations of corruption and mismanagement of inmates. Inmates like Jules (Nicky) Arnstein, the husband of actress Fanny Brice, used his connections on the outside to tell stories of unequal treatment amongst the inmates. Arnstein told of how under Biddle's stewardship, well-to-do inmates with large bank accounts could pay for and receive special favors. The bureau's policy that before an inmate could be paroled he had to be tested and cleared of syphilis led to accusations that the institution's doctor was charging $10 and up (dependent upon the inmate's monetary worth) for a clean bill of health. Overcrowded conditions had led to inmates working jobs that were traditionally held by staff. Allegations of inmates bribing officers for special favors abounded. Not even the chaplain's office was without controversy when it was discovered that a volunteer who had been supplying inmates with cigarettes was actually working in concert with a former inmate and bringing in cigarettes laced with morphine.

Also during this period, escapes and escape attempts were at an all-time high.[29] Inmate Herbert Bigelow, founder of the Brown and Bigelow Printing Company, had been working alongside inmate Charlie Ward in the prison's records office. The inmate taking mug shots was named George Kelly

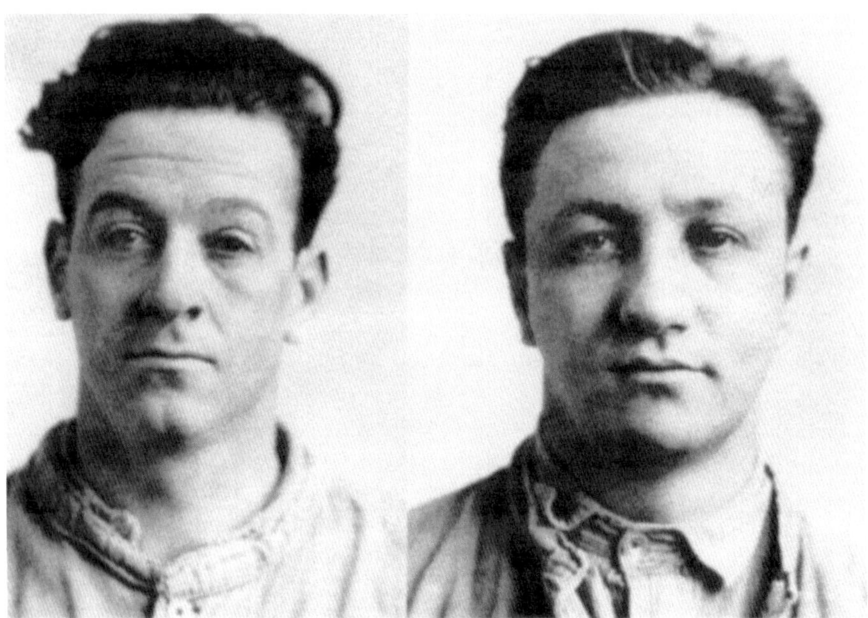

Thomas James Holden and Jimmy Keating were sentenced on April 17, 1928, for the 1926 robbery of the Grand Trunk Railroad mail car in Evergreen Park, Illinois. After securing trusty passes, both men escaped on September 28, 1930. *Courtesy National Archives and Records Administration.*

Barnes. During this time period and the time that followed, several inmates obtained trusty passes and were able to just walk away from the institution.

One such occasion involved inmates Thomas James Holden and Francis Keating. Both had been charged in the 1926 robbery of a Grand Trunk mail train at Evergreen Park, Illinois. Both had eluded capture until 1928, when a group, including former U.S. Representative Charles S. Wharton, managed to pull off an identical robbery of the same train. Holden and Keating were able to secure trusty passes and walked away from Leavenworth on February 28, 1930.

Inmate Frank Nash had been assigned to work as a cook in the prison's hospital. His charismatic personality—as well as his ability to cook—enabled him to make friends with the deputy warden, who had the responsibility of overseeing the hospital meals. Soon, Nash was granted a trusty's pass and served as the head cook at the deputy warden's house, which was located on the front lawn of the institution. On October 19, 1930, Nash approached the front gate and presented his trusty pass to the officer. At 9:00 p.m., the officer contacted the associate warden to advise him that Nash needed to return to the institution for count only to be told that Nash had not been there all evening.

Another escape that occurred on February 28, 1927, was most embarrassing.[30] Inmate John Carroll had been received at the institution on March 27, 1926, for forgery after being sentenced in the Northern District of Oklahoma. Carroll had been placed on a work assignment in the institution's factory, where he was tasked with building shipping crates. Enlisting the help of the assistant superintendent of industries, Charles Thompson, the inmate devised a plan in which he would construct a wooden box, measuring three by three by thirteen feet, in which he could be placed. The box would then be mixed in with other items being shipped out of the institution and then delivered to Thompson's residence. Carroll arrived as planned and found a set of new clothes, which he changed into prior to Thompson's return home. Realizing he had been double-crossed, the staff member went on the run and was captured three weeks later in New Orleans. When interviewed by police, Thompson admitted to helping Carroll in exchange for half of a reported $100,000 Carroll had hiding on the outside. For his troubles, all Thompson received was a prison sentence of fourteen years.

Two known escape attempts illustrate just how desperate an individual can be to gain his freedom. The mastermind of these escapes was named Morris "Red" Rudensky. Big Red, as he was known by his criminal associates, was an accomplished safecracker and expert escape artist. His history of escapes had insured that while he was at Leavenworth, his every move would be monitored. Red's plan called for him and another inmate to be shipped out of the institution's print shop in a packing crate with the regular shipment of goods. The print shop was in charge of printing documents and forms for other federal prisons and some government agencies. The crate they had their hearts set on was one destined for the federal prison at McNeil Island, Washington.

Both inmates had realized that getting themselves into the print shop after hours would be a daunting task and had devised a foolproof plan. They put this plan into motion four days before the escape. It called for both inmates to be placed in the institution's hospital, where little to no supervision occurred. Working in the print shop afforded the inmates the use of several tools. Red's choice to facilitate such an injury was the shop saw. As he sat working at the saw, he thought that he didn't want to lose a finger or a hand, so he decided the upper meaty part of his hand would have to do. Taking a deep breath, he pushed down on the starter button with his foot and shoved his hand into the saw blade. His coconspirator, described as an overweight inmate

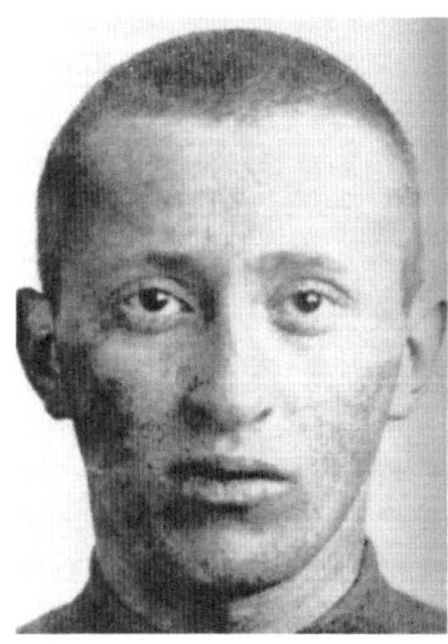

Morris "Red" Rudensky made several escape attempts on his own but declined a chance to join the others on December 11, 1931. *Courtesy National Archives and Records Administration.*

with asthma, took a less painful approach and feigned a heart attack. Both landed in the institution's hospital.

A few days later, just after the 4:00 a.m. count, Red and his partner placed linens in their beds, knowing that no one should notice until the 10:00 a.m. doctor's check. Making their way into the print shop was easy; Red, aside from being a safecracker, was also a locksmith and had made himself a set of keys. They hid themselves in the crate, and as the detail showed up for work, a couple of other inmates in the know nailed the top on the crate. The nails were coated with graphite, making it easier to remove them once the escapees were outside the walls.

In short order, the crate was loaded on the truck and headed for the rear gate. Inside the gate, officers began probing the crates with a pointed shiv, about 10 inches in length, connected to a long pole. The shiv managed to miss Red but went right through the foot of the other inmate. Shortly thereafter, the crate was again on the move, and once it arrived at the railroad station, it was loaded onto a train. Here's where the escape went south. Even though the crate was marked "this side up," it was placed on the train upside down. The size and weight of the crate made it impossible to open even with the graphite-tipped nails. As the train began moving, Red's accomplice began to bleed through the crate. Red recalls that before passing out, he imagined himself drowning in his partner's blood, which was running into his mouth and flooding his nostrils, making it impossible to breathe. His jubilation at escaping the walls of Leavenworth became prayers that the two would be discovered. Seven hours went by before a railroad expressman discovered blood running all over the floor beneath the crate. Both men were returned to the institution and suffered from dizzy spells and infections for weeks.

Rudensky's plans for a life outside the prison didn't stop there. Once back in his position at the print shop, he began taking notes on the operation of the hospital—particularly the operation of the morgue and how the dead bodies of inmates were handled. Usually, an inmate's dead body stayed no more than twenty-four hours in the morgue before it was shipped to either a local mortuary or released to the family. The institution never embalmed a body on site. Red discovered that one inmate died about every three weeks on average. The bodies were placed in canvas bags much like those used to bury sailors at sea. Without telling anyone of the plan, he enlisted the help of an orderly to give him a sign when an inmate was about to die, then another when he did die. Red advised the orderly that he was going to use the opportunity to smuggle out some information to his buddies. While he waited, he carved a pistol out of a piece of wood just in case his plan went south outside the institution. One afternoon, the orderly gave him the signal that an inmate was about to die. Red had also gained information that it was an older inmate suffering from a liver disease who had lost weight, thus creating enough room for two in the bag.

Finally, word came that the inmate had passed away at about 5:30 a.m., and it was time for Red to make his move. His plan called for him to talk to several inmates, telling a couple of them that he was going over to the laundry to talk with the foreman, then he advised two others he was going to the prison library after breakfast and a couple more that he was headed to the furnace room to apply for a job. This way, if any officers inquired, they would have a hard time locating him. Once in the hospital, he made his way to the morgue. After untying the sack, Red found it difficult to crawl into it with the dead body and even related that the body toppled to the floor several times. Once Red made it into the bag, he drew the drawstring, tying it from the inside and then pushing the strings out so as not to arouse suspicion.

Almost immediately, he began to heavily perspire inside the bag. Lying on his right side with his arm around the dead body's waist, Red became increasingly sick from the stench. The smell became unbearable, making the would-be escapee try mouth-breathing instead of breathing through his nostrils. About thirty minutes passed before Red heard any type of talking. It only took a matter of seconds for him to realize he had to give up his fight for freedom when he heard the words, "we're moving the body at noon." This would mean another four hours of hugging the dead man—a feat he couldn't imagine.

After the two orderlies left, Red began tearing at the drawstrings to gain his freedom. As he did so, he was confronted by the hospital orderly, who asked, "what in the hell are you doing, Red, trying to steal the poor slob's gold tooth?" Sick and unable to talk and almost at the point of throwing up, the mastermind regained his composure and began laughing. He abandoned his plan and made his way back to the yard, where news of his ordeal was spreading like a diarrhea epidemic.

During the summer of 1926, Mabel Walker Willebrandt, along with other ranking members of the Federal Prison Service, decided that it was time to make a change at Leavenworth. After they contacted FBI head J. Edgar Hoover, Hoover made a call to Thomas B. White. The plan called for White to be placed in the position of "acting" deputy warden, and once the heads of the FPS had convinced Warden W.I. Biddle to retire, White would be his replacement. It was also determined that White would retain his status as a special agent for the FBI. After several months of discussions with his wife, Bessie, whose main worry was raising their two young sons in the shadow of the largest federal prison in the country, Tom White accepted the offer and officially reported to the institution on October 1, 1926.

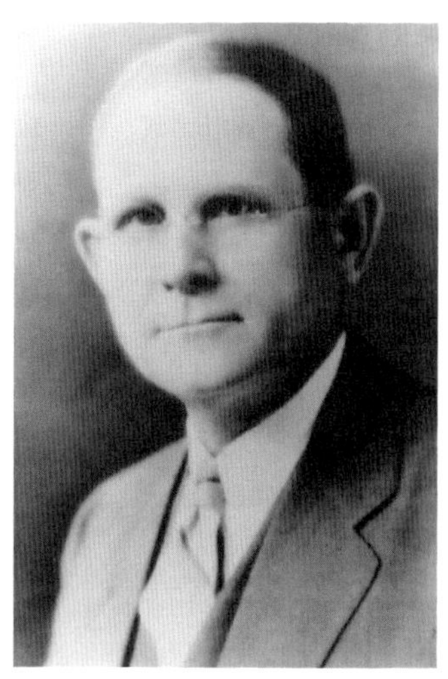

Official warden's photograph of Thomas B. White. *Courtesy of the author.*

After spending most of their lives in south and central Texas, the first challenge the White family faced was the bitter cold of the Kansas winter. Shortly after their arrival, many of the officers, inmates and townspeople began to survey Tom White. Here was a man over six feet tall, active in all that he did, seen strolling about the grounds without a heavy winter coat while going about his daily business of learning all there was to know about the institution. More than once, Bessie would hear, "look at that fool man out in this weather with no coat." After some prodding from his wife, Tom finally consented to wearing a suit of long woolen underwear in lieu of a heavy coat, for which, he argued, he had neither time nor patience.

With the retirement of Warden Biddle, the day was fast approaching that Tom White would be officially named the new warden. One hurdle to overcome in this process was the fact that never before had a Texas Democrat been appointed to any position while a Republican president resided in the White House. Hoover and White knew the significance of this and what it meant to the White family if Tom had been appointed on his birthday, which would be on March 6, 1927. To avoid any delays or last-minute reprisals, and fearing a congressional backlash over some alleged improprieties, they decided to wait for Congress to adjourn before the announcement became official. On March 7, 1927, special agent Thomas Bruce White officially became the warden of the United States Penitentiary, Leavenworth.

Now in charge of an institution and facing the same issues of overcrowding and understaffing, White realized his approach had to be different from that of his predecessor. He decided to take a hands-on approach and learn from his staff and inmate population. It wasn't uncommon to see the warden walking around the institution with an officer while asking questions.

One afternoon, while walking the grounds with an officer, the warden was asking questions when the officer abruptly stopped and pointed toward an inmate passing by and remarked, "see that convict over there, he's up to something he shouldn't be." Curiously, the warden began looking over the inmate and couldn't see anything in his appearance or mannerisms that aroused suspicion. He began questioning the officer as to what made him sure. Was it his appearance, actions, smell? The officer's reply was, "could be." The officer even offered the warden a bet based on whether or not he (the officer) was right. Passing on the wager, White called over the inmate and began questioning him, and still nothing about him raised suspicion. White's curiosity was in full swing, though, and he finally challenged the officer to prove his point. The officer directed the inmate into an empty office, where the officer began questioning the inmate as to what he had on him. The inmate continued to insist he had nothing until the officer directed him to submit to a strip search, and at this point, the con came clean—hidden on his person was a money belt loaded with cash.

Getting to know the inmate population was another issue. Numerous inmates had previously served time at Atlanta while White was there. They knew he was a no-nonsense type who advocated a firm and fair policy regarding inmates. White was also aware that every institution had its leaders amongst the inmate population—the one inmate who had the ability to organize and lead others. Leavenworth was no exception, and that one inmate was Morris "Red" Rudensky. It didn't take long for the warden to seek out Red. During a meeting with Rudensky, the warden laid it all on the table. Both men agreed that overcrowding and inadequate facilities were something they both had to handle. Promising no favors, the warden assured the inmate that he would do the best he could with what they both had to work with. Warden White conveyed to the inmate that he would do his best to ensure every inmate received fair treatment while making sure it was understood that the inmates themselves were responsible for the treatment they received.

6

RIOT, MURDER AND A HANGING

Through his efforts, Warden Tom White had gained a great deal of respect for and from the officers. During his tenure, two incidents occurred that would not only put White to the test but prove to all those around him, officer and inmate alike, that he truly was a man of his word. The first incident occurred on August 1, 1929.[31] Events leading up to that day included increased violence amongst the inmates as well as an increase in assaults on staff. The hot, dry summer, compounded by overcrowding, had led to a dramatic increase in violations of prison rules. Sensing more serious trouble was brewing, White, as well as his officers, began probing the inmate population for answers. When that failed, the warden invoked a crackdown on the inmate population by applying stricter rules and withholding regular privileges such as visitation and yard time.

On August 1, 1929, during the serving of the noon meal, inmates were pressed shoulder to shoulder in a dining room on a day during which temperatures broke 110 degrees. The meal consisted of seasoned Spanish rice and boiled potatoes. Between the hot seasoning of the meal, the temperature and unrest amongst the population, it didn't take long for something to break loose. By all recollections, the meal wasn't fit to feed, and if that wasn't bad enough, those who had eaten in the first wave had made their way out to the yard.

The unrest in the dining room began with a cup being thrown against the wall, then another, then plates of food and utensils were sent flying across the room.[32] Above the noise of approximately 1,900 violent inmates, one could be heard screaming, "You bastards can keep your slop!"

Inmates began beating two officers as a third was thrown to the ground and kicked and stomped. Inmates dived off of tables toward officers fighting for their lives. Almost simultaneously, fights began breaking out on the yard. One inmate was stabbed and another had his ear nearly bit off as the chaos and violence escalated. Inmates began storming the kitchen area, destroying everything along the way. They began grabbing knives, meat cleavers and fashioning weapons out of anything they could get their hands on. Officers armed with rifles and shotguns, above the fray on the gun gallery, were rendered all but useless for fear of injuring fellow officers. Suddenly, from out of nowhere, Warden White appeared followed by Deputy Warden Fred Zerbst and Father Kaline, the prison chaplain. Amidst the ever increasing violence, calls of "kill the dirty bastards and let's string them up right here" could be heard.

White and Zerbst made their way through the angry mob amid the chaos and weapons being thrust about their heads. The chaplain had begun pleading with Red Rudensky to help stop the madness, only to hear the reply, "It's not my doing, father, and I'm damned tired of being blamed for everything. Since I'm always catching hell, I might as well enjoy the fun!" Unnerved and showing unusual courage, White found Rudensky and asked, "What is it these men want? Tell me and maybe I can straighten it

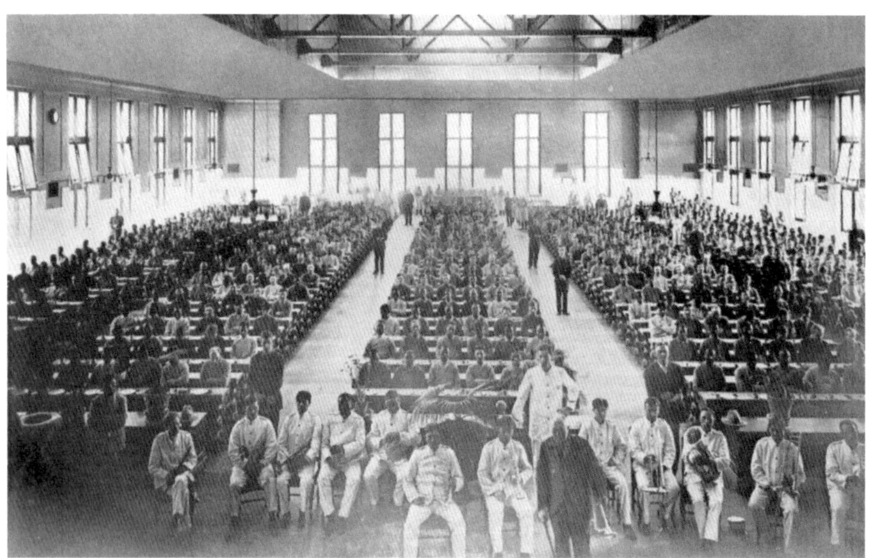

Music calms the savage beast. The inmate orchestra is pictured in the front center of the dining room at USP Leavenworth. *Courtesy of the author.*

out." Before Red could give an answer, another convict screamed, "Let the warden have it, him and his god-damned sisters!" Almost as quickly, another lifer named Henderson looked at Red and loudly stated, "Tell them what we all want, Red. If they don't give it to us then let's chop them up for a snack, but give them a chance."

As the noise level diminished, Rudensky climbed up on a nearby table, pleading with the rioters, "Listen, guys, listen a second. Let me give the pitch to the man. If he doesn't accept our deal, then let somebody else get up here." Red began by stating, "Warden, we want our mail and visiting privileges back immediately." As a crowd of inmates circled around the warden and his associates, Red continued, "We've got to have some decent grub and some decent cooks, this shit isn't worth feeding pigs and you know it. Either get us some decent grub or we'll tear this place apart. We don't deserve this slop and you can't expect a man to live on it." Standing his ground and staring Red in the eyes, White replied, "You've just made a bargain. Tell the men to ease off and I'll look into the food situation right now. You can have all your privileges back, too, but first get your men back into their cells."

After a few seconds, Red called out to the crowd, "Knock it off, the man says we'll get new food and our privileges. White's never crossed us; let's give him a chance." The rioters disbanded and headed to their cells. Amongst those leaving, many were still voicing distrust and anger, but not one con laid hands on the warden or his men.

After clearing the mess hall, the officers were left to contend with the crowd on the yard, and unrest amongst the cell houses could still be heard all along Metropolitan Avenue in front of the institution. Officers who had been fighting the crowd on the yard used fire hoses until they were overtaken and the hoses were turned on them. Suddenly, a shot rang out from one of the east gate towers, and the bullet struck a convict with a weapon. Inmates began making their way toward the cell houses en masse, joining others who were refusing to return to their cells. Entering B cell house, Warden White and a shotgun team made their way to the light side, and as they turned the corner in front of the cells, an inmate in the first cell attempted to trip the warden. This was met with a ringing shotgun blast that removed the inmate's foot and sent other inmates toward the nearest cell. Inmate Mike Martinez made the mistake of peering over the second-floor railing to see what had happened and was met with a shot to his head. Over the course of the next twenty-four hours, the sounds of screams, discontent and gunshots could be heard coming from the institution. After calm was returned amongst the

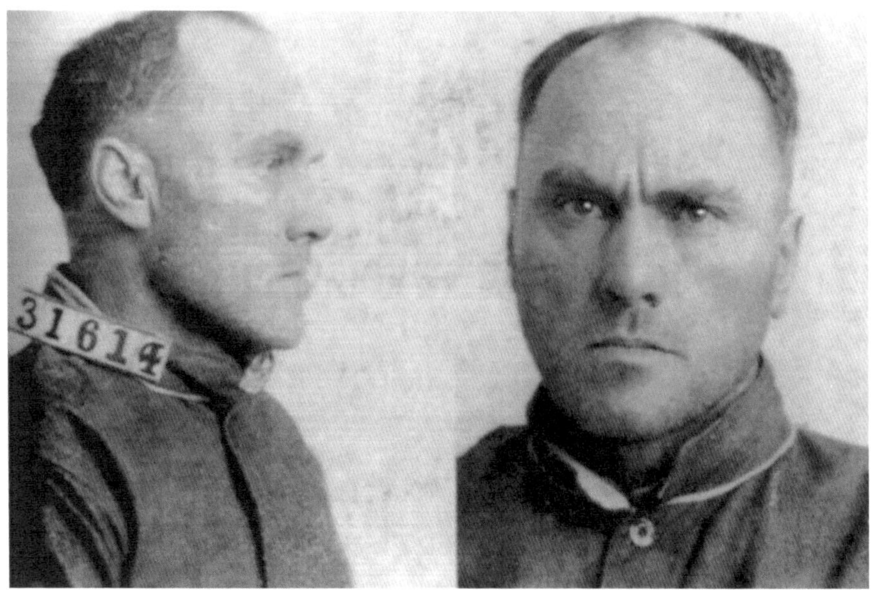

Serial killer Carl Panzram's only regret in life: "That the human race have but one neck and I can't get my hands around it." *Courtesy National Archives and Records Administration.*

population, local newspapers reported that one inmate was dead and three suffered serious injuries.

During Warden White's career, he had held to a belief that those incarcerated differed very little from those who were not. He believed that inside of everyone there existed good and bad. Not that he believed those inside the prison didn't belong there, but maybe some who were incarcerated weren't as lucky as some who were not. On February 1, 1929, as White sat in his office looking through the open door as new arrivals were marched into the institution, he first saw a man that personified, both in appearance and manner, the qualities of a person of pure evil and ruthlessness. Upon inquiring, he learned that the inmate in question was suspected of killing several people, some in the most heinous ways possible. The inmate's name was Carl Panzram.

As the in-processing of the Washington (D.C.) Asylum and Jail inmates was taking place, the jail's superintendent, William L. Peak, had the opportunity to speak with Warden White and Deputy Warden Zerbst. During this conversation, Peak spoke of Panzram's dangerous character and violent history. Peak's advice was to immediately place Panzram in isolation. Following his in-processing, during which he was issued the number 31614 and outfitted with a grey uniform, Panzram was led to Building 63, the isolation building, where he met with Deputy Warden Zerbst. After receiving a stern lecture about what was expected of new inmates, the rules and regulations and his job assignment in the laundry, Panzram was asked by Zerbst if he had anything to say. His reply was, "I'll kill the first man that bothers me."

For his first few months in Leavenworth, Panzram kept to himself, reading books from the institution library, and spoke very little. His official inmate file only indicates one infraction of institution rules that occurred when he was charged with trafficking. The incident involved Panzram giving another inmate eight packs of Camel cigarettes and four bags of Bull Durham tobacco. What he exchanged those items for is not noted in his file. When asked where he came about the tobacco, his reply was, "I don't care to tell."

It was while Panzram was awaiting a hearing on these charges that he would commit his final murder. In his official statement, Warden Tom White states that he arrived at the institution and entered his office on June 20, 1929, between 7:50 and 7:55 a.m. His attention was drawn to Officer Dave Watkins, who entered the office exclaiming, "Inmate Carl Panzram has just killed Mr. Warnke and is running amok!" White immediately secured a pistol from the armory officer and entered the institution en route to the west yard, where the laundry building is located. As White made his way down the corridor, an inmate passed and advised him that Panzram had made his way to the east yard; upon hearing this, White thought Panzram was on his way toward the brickyard portion of the institution. After White arrived at the brickyard, the foreman in charge advised the warden that he had not seen Panzram. As White was making his way toward the west yard area, he was advised by another inmate that Panzram had surrendered and was placed in isolation. Once Panzram's capture and Warnke's death were confirmed, White notified the superintendent of federal prisons.

Officer Phil Holtgraves was on duty inside the laundry building at the time of the murder. In his official report, the officer observed Panzram walk into the laundry and head toward his work area.[33] As he was writing passes to other inmates, Holtgraves stated, "I heard a disturbance, and when I looked toward that area, I saw Panzram with an iron bar. As I ran toward Panzram, he immediately began chasing another inmate, who passed the laundry foreman R.G. Warnke who was lying on the floor. Panzram raised the bar and struck Mr. Warnke."

Inmates began running out of the laundry, followed by Panzram, who was still in possession of the iron bar. Holtgraves followed and says that Panzram

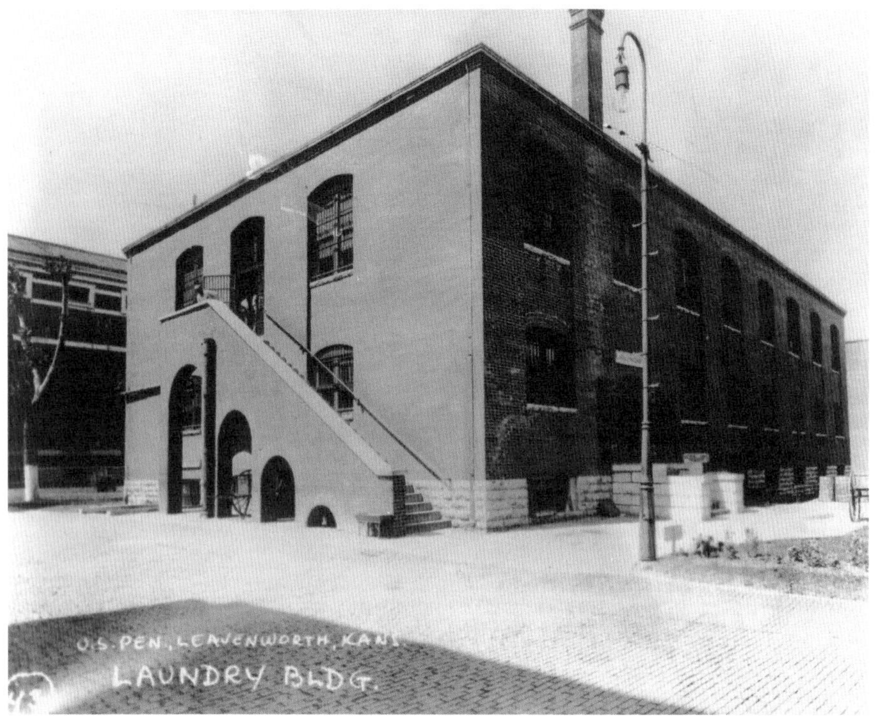

The oldest building inside the prison is the laundry building. The first floor housed the laundry and the second contained the clothing department. The basement housed the A cell house shower room and the vault. Carl Panzram murdered laundry foreman R.G. Warnke inside and was executed just steps away. *Courtesy of the author.*

ran across to the deputy warden's office and came out a few seconds later. At this time, Panzram began chasing Officer Louis B. Guenther. Guenther states that once Panzram gave chase, he ran toward the east gate towers to alert the officers there, who drew their weapons. Panzram, realizing what the officer was up to, took refuge behind a couple of boxcars on the tracks in front of the powerhouse. After briefly chasing another inmate, Panzram returned to the deputy warden's office, where he was met by several officers. He immediately dropped the bar, proclaiming, "I guess that's all I can get," and surrendered.

Over the course of the next fifteen months, Panzram was housed in the segregation portion of Building 63. In December 1929, a grand jury was empaneled at Kansas City, Missouri, followed by a jury trial held in Topeka in April 1930. In both the grand jury hearing and the trial, seven staff members and nine prisoners testified about the horrendous events of that day. It was also during this period that the media reported on the victims of Panzram. A manuscript had emerged that was purportedly credited to the inmate. White had ordered Panzram's mail monitored, and it was noticed that he was corresponding with an individual named Henry James. Upon further investigation, it was discovered that James was actually a jailer named Henry Lesser who worked at the Washington (D.C.) Asylum and Jail. It was court-ordered that Panzram would undergo a psychiatric evaluation to be conducted by Dr. Karl Menninger.

On April 16, 1930, Panzram stood before the District Court of Kansas, First Division, charged with violating Sections 273 and 275 of the U.S. Penal Code (murder in the first degree and capital murder on government lands).[34] The jury foreman handed the following statement to the judge after jury deliberations: "We the jury in the above entitled case, duly impaneled and sworn, upon our oath, find the defendant guilty as charged in the indictment herein, signed O.A. Kirkendall, Foreman." Panzram, through his attorney, asked that each juror be polled, and thereupon, each confirmed the verdict. Without delay, judge Richard J. Hopkins, inquiring if the defendant had any comments for the court, received the reply, "I have nothing to say."

> *"Therefore, is now here by the court considered, ordered, and adjudged that said Carl Panzram be remanded to the custody of the warden of the United States Penitentiary at Leavenworth, Kansas, and by said warden kept in solitary confinement in said penitentiary until Friday, September 5, 1930 and that on that date between the hours of 6 a.m. And 9 a.m. the said Carl Panzram be by the United States Marshal for the District of Kansas, taken to some suitable place within the walls of said United States Penitentiary and then and there hanged by the neck until he is dead. Signed, Richard J. Hopkins, Judge."*

During the months leading up to the execution, Warden White took it upon himself to frequently talk with the condemned man. The warden asked Panzram if there were any specific requests, and Panzram replied, "I don't want any of the god-damned chaplains around during the hanging; it's none of their damned business, and I have no use for them." A week before the execution date, White ordered the windows of all the cell houses and dormitories be whitewashed so as to prevent inmates from viewing the execution. On the morning of September 5, officers in Building 63 reported to the warden that Panzram was refusing to exit his cell and inquired if they should use force. White told them that he would personally take care of it.

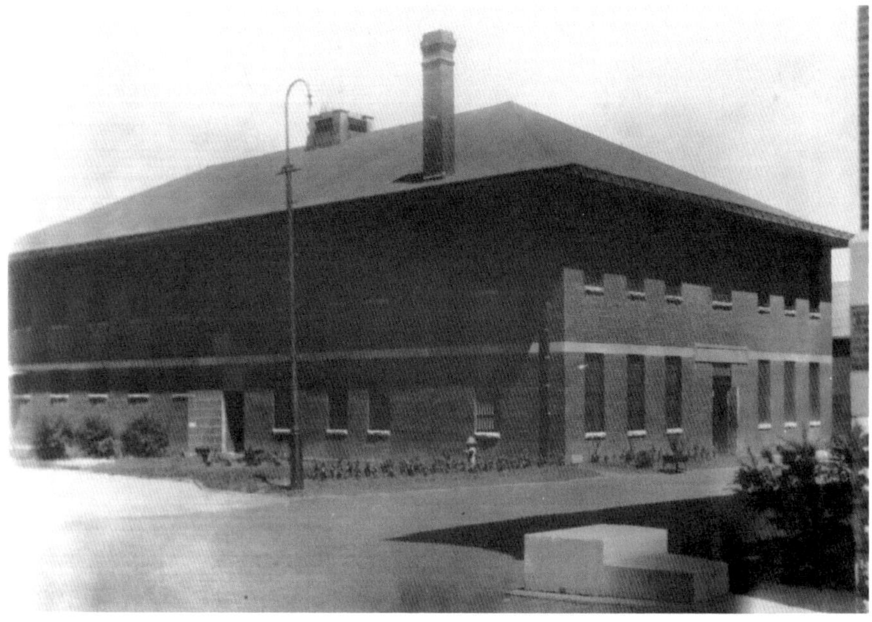

Building 63 originally housed the deputy warden's office and segregation. The isolation building was a separate building behind this one. The small courtyard separating this building and the laundry building is where inmate Carl Panzram was executed. *Courtesy of the author.*

Upon entering the cell, White advised the condemned man, "This is your party and you've got to be there. You have two choices. You can either walk out there like a man, or you can be taken my way." Panzram replied, "I told you I didn't want those god-damned chaplains out there. I'll come as soon as you get them out of here!" Minutes after the chaplains departed, Panzram ascended the gallows. As he stood awaiting the rope and hood, he shouted, "All right you sons a bitches, you've come to see a show and now you're gonna see it. They tell me when I drop and hit the end of this rope I'll crap my pants. I just wish I could take them off so I could crap all over you dirty bastards!" As the noose was adjusted, Panzram stared his executioner in the face and proclaimed, "Hurry it up you Hoosier bastard, I could kill ten men while you're screwing around!"

Panzram's official death certificate, signed by U.S. Public Health Service representative Dr. Justin Fuller, lists the cause of death as "dislocation of the cervical vertebrae and strangulation." Panzram's body was removed from the institution and is in an unmarked grave in the prison's cemetery, aptly named Peckerwood Hill.[35]

7

DECEMBER 11, 1931

Shortly after the August 1929 riot, the United States Disciplinary Barracks at Fort Leavenworth was turned over to the Federal Prison Service and began operation as a federal prison annex. Deputy Warden Fred Zerbst was appointed warden of the institution, which immediately helped with the overcrowding issue at the main facility. Amongst its population were inmates confined on narcotics-related crimes. The establishment of the Federal Bureau of Prisons on May 19, 1930, brought about several changes in the way prisons operated. The new director, Sanford Bates, quickly instilled a strict code of secrecy. Before, the daily happenings at federal prisons appeared in local and national newspapers as well as magazines and other periodicals. This new code of secrecy was intended to eliminate that. This caused major dissent with the media, because up until this time, they could merely call the institution and receive updates. Now, nothing could be released until it was approved by the new director.

Friday morning, December 11, 1931, began cold and gray. Overnight, a steady rain had fallen, adding to the unusually heavy rains that had fallen that month and causing a bone-chilling cold to settle over the area. Life in and out of the institution was much the same. Inmates were awakened at 5:30 a.m. as usual and began the day by making their beds and cleaning their cells before they were marched off to the dining room for breakfast at 6:00 a.m. Many residents, as well as the day shift officers, were up and tending to their morning rituals unaware that both worlds were on a collision course. With the breakfast meal ended, Warden White was concluding his morning rounds of the institution and headed back to his office by 8:30 a.m. His morning routine included meetings with inmates starting at 9:00 a.m. sharp. His first meeting that morning was with Fred Barker, member of the Ma Barker Gang (and son of Kate "Ma" Barker).

At the conclusion of the morning meal, every inmate was formed up in ranks by 7:15 a.m., and detail officers marched them to their respective job sites. Inmate Will Green (No. 17242) was assigned to the clothing department on the second floor of the laundry building. Grover C. Durrill (No. 20772) and Tom Underwood (No. 31852) were both assigned to the main institution hospital annex, Stanley Brown (No. 22473) worked in the plumbing and tin shop, Earl Thayer (No. 20768) worked on the fourth floor of the shoe factory, George Curtis (No. 20773) was assigned as the "first aid man" on the third floor in a private office of the prison shoe factory and Charles Berta (No. 39571) was assigned to the steel construction crew building the new east wing of the industries building. Durrill, Thayer and Curtis had been convicted, along with Frank Nash, in the Okesa train robbery. Green was convicted of robbing a post office and assaulting a mail messenger in Kansas City, Kansas, and sentenced on January 16, 1922. His temper had earned him a reputation as a violent offender capable of murder. Underwood's extensive criminal history included robbing mail trains and banks, and he was serving a twenty-five-year sentence for kidnapping a mail clerk in Hibbing, Minnesota, in 1927. Berta, a relative newcomer, had been sentenced in September 1931 in San Francisco for robbing the mail and assault upon a mail carrier and had been received at Leavenworth on October 4.

Once the inmates reach their job assignments, accountability is vulnerable. Detail supervisors are busy giving instructions and getting the shop operations up and running, while officers are busy writing passes, issuing tools and taking care of other job necessities. This would have been the perfect time for the escapees to gather, get their weapons[36] and make last-second decisions and preparations before they put their plan into motion.

At approximately 9:10 a.m., Durrill, Curtis and Underwood had made their way to the area of the institution where the main corridor connects to the dining room and the auditorium area known as the rear corridor.[37] After they presented passes to Officer Louis M. Kelly, the officer opened the gate, giving the three inmates access to the main corridor. As Kelly was securing the gate, Curtis immediately jammed a pistol into the stomach of Officer Kelly and ordered him to back up against the wall. As Curtis held the officer hostage, Durrill and Underwood hurriedly made their way toward the warden's office. Stripping Officer Kelly of his keys, Curtis passed

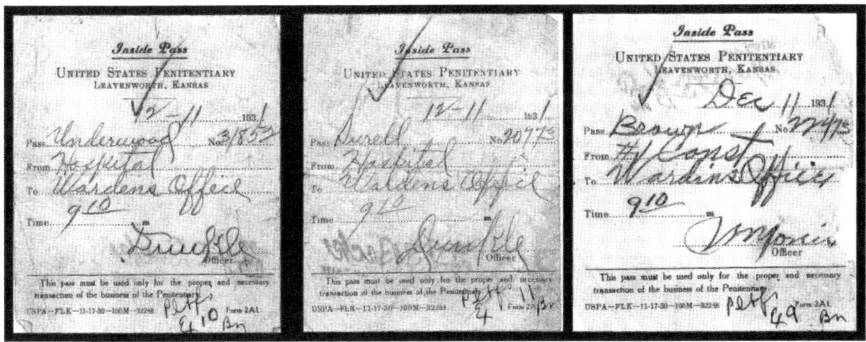
Inside Pass
UNITED STATES PENITENTIARY
LEAVENWORTH, KANSAS
12-11 1931
Pass Underwood No. 31853
From Hospital
To Wardens Office
Time 9:10 m
Officer
This pass must be used only for the proper and necessary transaction of the business of the Penitentiary.
USPA—FLK—11-17-30—100M—32288 Form 2AL

Inside Pass
UNITED STATES PENITENTIARY
LEAVENWORTH, KANSAS
12-11 1931
Pass Durell No.
From Hospital
To Wardens Office
Time 9:10 m
Officer
This pass must be used only for the proper and necessary transaction of the business of the Penitentiary.
USPA—FLK—11-17-30—100M—32288 Form 2AL

Inside Pass
UNITED STATES PENITENTIARY
LEAVENWORTH, KANSAS
Dec 11 1931
Pass Brown No.
From #1 Const office
To Wardens Office
Time 9:10 m
Officer
This pass must be used only for the proper and necessary transaction of the business of the Penitentiary.
USPA—FLK—11-17-30—100M—32288 Form 2AL

Found in the original trial transcripts are the forged passes used by Underwood, Durrill and Brown to gain access to the main corridor and the warden's office. *Courtesy National Archives and Records Administration.*

them through the bars of the door to the other four inmates—Berta, Thayer, Brown and Green. Unable to open the door from the outside, they passed the keys back to Curtis, who opened the door to allow the remaining four into the main corridor.

Upon entering the outer area of the warden's office, Underwood, armed with an Auto & Burglar shotgun, and Durrill, armed with a Winchester .30-30 rifle, ordered the warden's secretary, E.A. Echtold, and his two clerks to stand up and get against the wall. Upon hearing the commotion happening in the outer office, White stood up at his desk and, realizing what was happening, took his car keys from his pocket and tossed them under his desk, then covered them with an area rug. Suddenly, he found himself staring down the barrel of the rifle and hearing the order, "Get out here now!" Following orders, the warden walked into the outer office just as Officer Kelly was being shoved through the door and was followed by four additional inmates. Forcing the hostages across the hall and into the chief clerk's office, the inmates took Mr. Wise, chief clerk; C.M. Scott, a civilian clerk; Ed Anthony, prison construction foreman; and J.E. Smith and E.L. Dugger, representatives of the Underwood Typewriter Company of Kansas City, as additional hostages.

As the inmates and hostages gathered in the chief clerk's office, Underwood gave Officer Kelly an order to call the warden's residence and have his car brought to the front of the institution. After fumbling about for what seemed to be an eternity, Kelly was able to convince the inmates that he did not know the number nor was he able to find it in the prison phone directory. Deciding too much time had already been wasted, the seven inmates and their hostages made their way to the main gate of the institution. As they approached the gate area, they encountered Mrs. R.B. Hershey and her daughter Nedetta Rothgeb. Rothgeb later stated that one of the inmates told her and her mother, "We won't hurt you, don't be afraid. Just get over there in the corner and keep still."

As they all headed toward the main entrance of the prison, Underwood pointed the shotgun into the face of Officer J.H. Dempsey and said, "Open the damn door!" Dempsey, an older officer, replied, "I'll be damned if I will. Only one man in this institution can make me unlock this door, and that is Warden White." Curtis produced multiple sticks of dynamite taped together with fuses and blasting caps and said, "If this gate isn't opened by the time I light this fuse, I'll blow all of us to hell!" As Curtis struck a match, Thayer threatened, "You'll be dead and in hell in a second if you don't open this door!" Dempsey replied, "I guess we'll all see each other in hell, then." Realizing such a disaster could result in a larger mass escape, Warden White approached Dempsey and calmly stated, "All right officer, open the door."

As the door swung open, the inmates shoved the hostages out first as they stripped the keys from Dempsey and locked the door behind them. The main tower officer immediately swung into action, removing a tarp from a Browning belt-fed machine gun and taking aim. Brown shouted, "If he fires, we'll kill you all. Order him to hold it." Warden White, again remaining calm, advised the tower officer not to shoot, explaining, "we've made it this

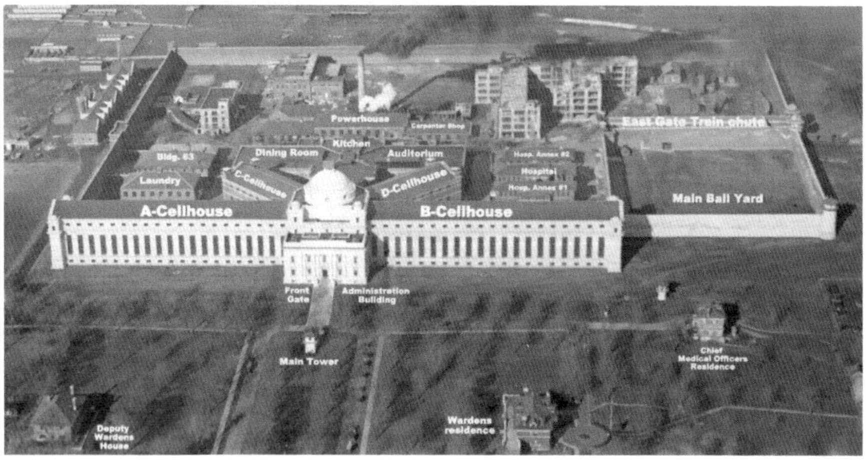

Aerial view of USP Leavenworth taken a few days after the escape. *Courtesy of the author.*

far—no reason for bloodshed now." As they made their way down the forty-three stairs of the institution, all seven of the inmates began a mad dash across the lawn toward the warden's residence with White in tow, leaving the rest of the hostages at the base of the main tower. A shot rang out from the armory, where Officer Hubert Gray had taken aim. Durrill yelled for the other inmates to keep going as he dropped to a knee to return fire. Officer Dempsey pleaded for the shooting to stop. As the inmates and Warden White made it to the garage that contained the warden's car, White advised the escapees that he had left the keys in his office, and there was not a spare set.

Bessie White had seen what was happening and, along with the chauffeur, took refuge in the kitchen of the residence. As the developments in the garage turned into a mad dash for Metropolitan Avenue, Bessie gave chase, but when she realized she was making things worse, she returned to the house and placed a call to the captain's office.

As the hostage-takers and Warden White headed toward the road, a bus was pulling up at the stop adjacent to the warden's driveway. The escapees' initial reaction was to board the bus, taking the driver and all aboard as additional hostages. In a split second, plans changed as inmate Curtis saw an approaching sedan headed east. Suddenly, the deafening blare of the institution's powerhouse whistle hastened their dash toward the sedan and freedom. After overpowering the car and ordering the driver to stop, Curtis and Thayer drew down on the occupants, demanding that they get out of the car. Five black soldiers—Sergeant Will Knox, Sergeant William Washington, Corporal Sidney A. Wilson, Corporal John Costly and Private Edgar N. Frye—from Fort Leavenworth occupied the Oakland Eight sedan. Overwhelmed, the Buffalo Soldiers exited the vehicle. As the inmates and the warden climbed on board, they discovered five more shotguns and several boxes of ammunition.

Berta took the wheel and immediately swung the vehicle around to head west. Berta asked the warden which way was the best road out of town. White advised the driver that if he took a right and followed the highway toward Atchison, they could be there within thirty minutes, cross the bridge into Missouri and make their getaway. Figuring he was being lied to, Berta made a sharp left turn. As the vehicle completed the turn, the pavement gave way to mud, and the vehicle immediately slid off the road into a ditch, almost overturning.

Desperation was beginning to mount as the escapees climbed out of the car. They made a mad dash toward the first house they saw, where a car was sitting outside of it. Unable to gain entry into the car, one of the inmates alerted his companions of an approaching car. Once again overwhelming the driver with drawn weapons, they recognized Officer Joe Kressin, who was responding to the emergency, and ordered him out of the car. Forcing White into the car, three of the inmates climbed inside while the other four mounted the running boards. The weak suspension, coupled with the weight of the occupants, made the vehicle sink into the deep mud. Turning west onto Mount Olivet Road, the inmates followed the winding road past the old Jewish Cemetery, out to Highway 33 and then to Dakota Road.

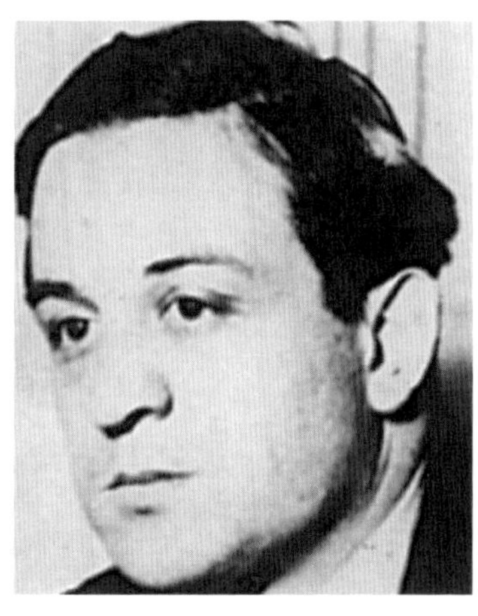

Charlie Berta was chosen as a last-minute replacement for the getaway driver who had learned he was going to be paroled within the next few months. *Courtesy of the author.*

Taking notice of a sedan, the inmates pulled up in front of what they believed was a rural farmhouse. Upon entering the building, they discovered they were at the Glen Valley School, locally known as the Possum Hollow School. Three of the escapees entered the school, one armed with the rifle while the other two wielded pistols. The twenty-five startled students jumped up from their desks. As some began to cry, others made a mad dash for the door, only to be met with the man with the rifle ordering, "get back and sit down, we won't hurt you." Turning his attention to the teacher, Anna Mayer, he said, "Look, lady, all I want is the keys to your car!" Mayer replied, "Go on about your business, boys. That car out there is the only thing I have. Go on and steal one from one of the farmers, I'm just a poor schoolteacher."

As he made his way toward a nearby table, the inmate said, "Come on now, get those keys." He picked up the teacher's purse, and as he rifled through it, Mayer exclaimed, "Put that down, I'm just a poor teacher!" The inmate replied, "Give me the keys and be quick about it." She replied, "I'll give you the keys if you give me my purse." Once the inmate had the keys in hand, the group headed out to the car. Unaware that the teacher's car had a push-button starter switch mounted under the dash, the inmates failed to start the car. Giving up, they mounted the running boards of Officer Kressin's car, and off they went. As the car pulled away, Mayer told two of the older boys to go out the back and follow the hedgerow up the hill to the nearby neighbor's house and let them know what had happened.

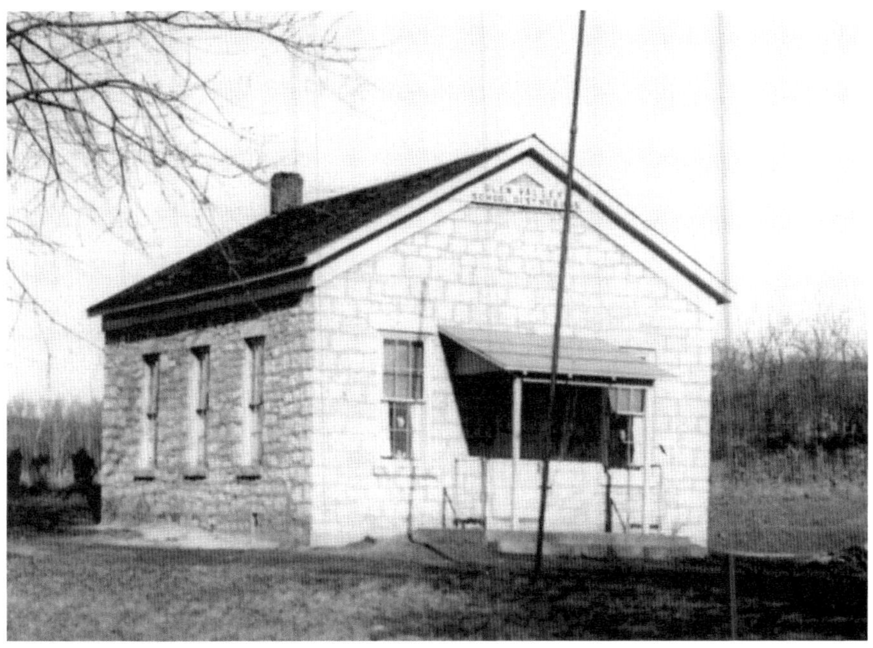

The Glen Valley School, locally known as the Possum Hollow School, was where the escapees encountered their first standoff. Schoolteacher Anna Mayer refused to surrender her car keys until the inmates gave back her purse. *Courtesy of the author.*

Back at the institution, off-duty officers were arriving and making their way to the armory, where they were outfitted with weapons and ammunition. Day captains and lieutenants began calling local law enforcement as well as the penitentiary annex at Fort Leavenworth. Officers inside the institution who had tried to respond to the front of the institution soon discovered that the door leading to the main corridor was locked, and the officer was nowhere to be found. Several made a dash for the east gate, where they could exit the institution and make their way to the front. Others attempted to get the inmates back to their cells. Inmates at first passively disobeyed orders but then became more aggressive.

As he arrived at the main institution, annex warden Fred Zerbst was accompanied by Major General Stuart Heintzleman, the post commander of Fort Leavenworth, as well as two companies of infantry soldiers. After being advised of the escape and the current situation of unrest inside the prison, Zerbst briefly spoke with Major General Heintzleman. The general ordered that a perimeter be set up around the institution. This consisted of three man machine-gun crews spread out across the front lawn. Two platoons of soldiers were dispatched to the east gate. The fully armed platoons marched into the institution to aid in locking down the prison. As the inmates realized what was happening, they began moving toward the cell houses. The remaining soldiers, along with all available staff, joined the hunt for the escapees.

With each passing minute, the seven desperate escapees continued on their quest for freedom. Simultaneously, the posse of armed men grew in numbers. Anyone who knew the terrain and owned a gun joined in the search. Every home that owned a phone provided updates. Leavenworth Police and county sheriff's officers, prison officers and military personnel gave chase. Army planes from the nearby Sherman Army Air Field, as well as local flyers, joined the search from the air. Even the numbers of curious onlookers swelled. In all, the media estimated that well over one thousand people took to the county road and farmer's field.

As the escapees and their hostage traveled across County Road 33, the car continued to get bogged down under the weight and by the muddy conditions of the road. After turning left onto what they believed to be another county road, the vehicle came to an abrupt stop. Sinking ever deeper, the vehicle would move no farther. Abandoning the car, the group began making their way up the road on foot and found a farmhouse just off the road in a shallow bluff.

Andy Haas was standing on his front porch when he noticed the men approaching the house. Inside the home were his son Leo and his daughters Rose and Clara, along with their neighbor Leo Forge. Stepping just inside the door, Andy said, "There's a group of hunters coming, and there's a whole bunch of them." As Andy turned around, the group forced him back through the door and entered the home. At this point, Rose stated that they immediately knew something was wrong when they noticed one of the men was wearing a suit.[38] One of the inmates tied the warden's hands behind his back and forced him to sit in a chair. All seven inmates began storming through the house demanding to know where the phone was. The family tried to convince them there was no phone, but the desperate men continued ransacking each room, insisting they were lying. At one point, one of the inmates noticed he had a broken shoelace and asked the young Rose if they had another. As she opened the drawer of a cabinet, another inmate, not knowing what was going on, slammed his pistol into the young girl's ribs, demanding, "Close that drawer!"

Convinced there was no phone, one of the inmates began questioning Andy about how to get to the nearest road. He explained that Highway

92 was directly south about a mile or so. The inmates ordered Andy to gather up the family and told them that they were going along on the walk. Andy began pleading with them, advising that his daughter Rose had just undergone an appendectomy a few weeks earlier and couldn't walk that far. One of the inmates commented, "Then we'll carry her." Rose replied, "Oh, no; I'll walk." As the hostages and escapees made their way toward the barn, an airplane flying low above the tree line startled the group. The inmates forced their hostages into the barn until the airplane was out of sight.

As they continued down a narrow winding cow path, Leo Haas stepped out of line, which was met with a strike from the butt of a rifle and an order to "get back in line and stay there!" As they came upon a clearing, they saw the farmhouse of Joe Gates a short distance away. Forcing their way into the Gates home, they found Joe and his wife and their son Joe Jr; their daughter Elizabeth Phillips; and her husband, Herschel, in the sitting room next to the wood-burning stove. As Joe Gates Sr. made his way to the doorway, one of the inmates stated, "We're revenue officers, and we're looking for a still!" The elder Gates replied, "Do your damndest!"

The inmates began going from room to room in search of a phone. Upon locating it, they tore it from the wall and threw it to the floor. Elizabeth began to doubt the story of the group being revenue officers when a low-flying plane again startled them. Thayer must have suspected she knew when he stated, "There's liable to be some shooting" as he directed the group down into the basement. Pointing to Elizabeth and Leo Forge, he said, "You two come along; we're going to find a still, and we want you to guide us."

As the group of escapees gathered with their three hostages, frustration had finally set in. The inmates argued amongst themselves as to their next move. Forcing their hostages out of the house, the group headed south through a cornfield. After a few anxious moments, Herschel Phillips emerged from the basement and began to follow. As they were nearing the edge of the field, one of the inmates noticed a prison officer on horseback; he also noticed Herschel. One of the convicts pointed a pistol toward the young man and began shouting, "Tell that officer to travel before we bump him!" Herschel immediately turned toward the Gates house and ran.

As they entered the roadway of Highway 92, Green and Thayer held onto the warden and ordered the others to hide behind a hedgerow. It wasn't too long before they spotted a Chevrolet Coupe headed west. As they had done with the other cars they hijacked, inmates Green, Thayer, Durrill and Curtis overwhelmed the four occupants of the vehicle, pointing their weapons and demanding, "Stop the car!"

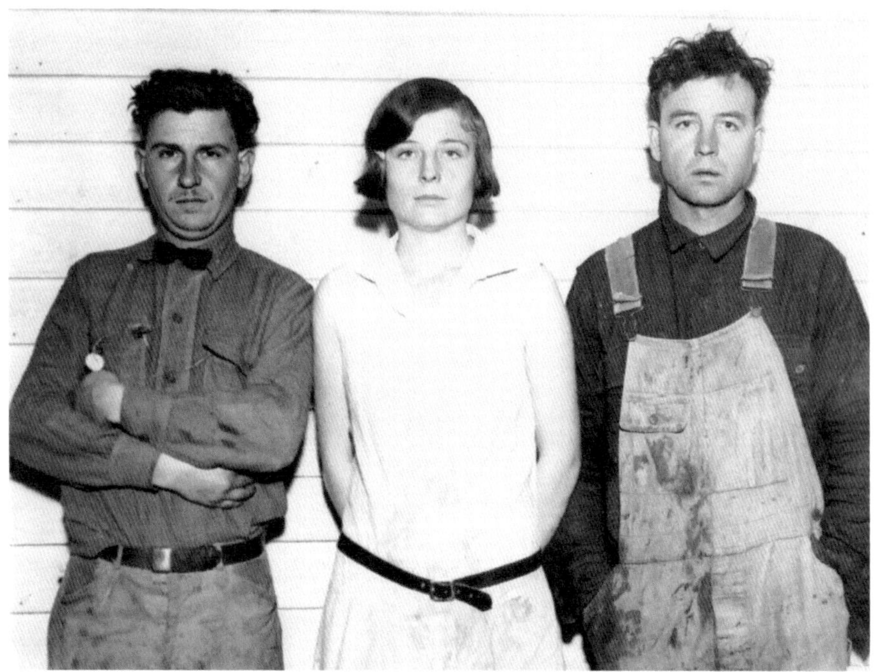

Left to right: Herschel Phillips; his wife, Elizabeth; and Joe Gates Jr. were all taken hostage at the Joe Gates farm. *Courtesy of the author.*

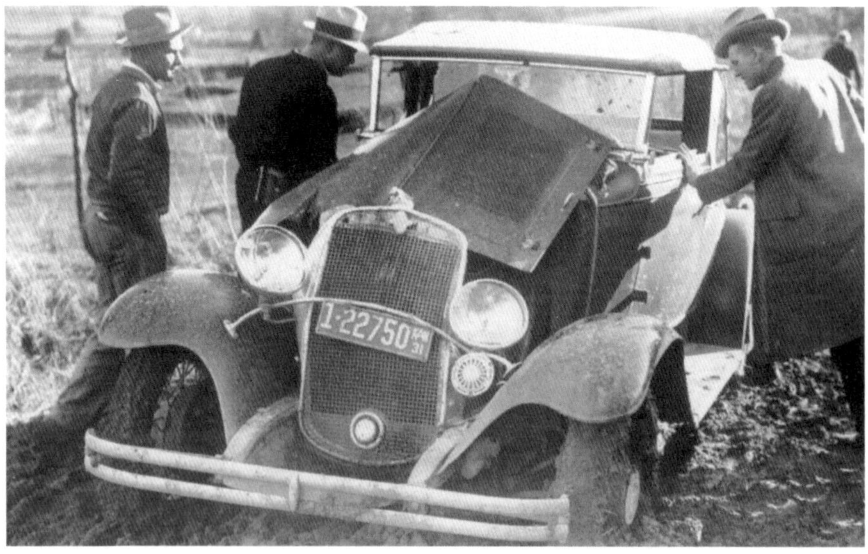

The last ride of Will Green, George Curtis and Grover C. Durrill. Riddled with bullets and damaged from running into a horse, the car became stuck in the mud on the road leading up to the Salisbury Farm. *Courtesy of the author.*

The occupants—twenty-two-year-old Carl Laufer, twenty-year-old Carl Bauer, nineteen-year-old Lyle Haite and eighteen-year-old Jack Gallivan—had heard about the prison break and were out looking for all the excitement. Little did they realize they were going to find it!

Once the vehicle came to a complete stop, Green, armed with a shotgun, desperately ordered, "Stick 'em up and get out of the car!" Realizing the vehicle was a two-seat coupe with a rumble seat, Green told the other three inmates, "Shake out and find another car." As the four boys made their way out of the car, Green shouted, "Get down the road and don't look back!" As they headed down the road, Warden White commented, "Don't cross them up, boys; these men are desperate." At the top of the ridge, inmate Thayer again saw an officer on horseback. He ordered White to "motion him to come on down here." The officer disappeared once again. Glancing about, Thayer saw Bauer turn and look over his shoulder and immediately raised his rifle. Warden White grabbed hold of the rifle and yelled for Elizabeth Phillips and Leo Forge to make a run for it, which they did as he wrestled with the inmate for control of the weapon. Thayer yelled at Green, "He's got the rifle!" Green raised the shotgun and delivered a crashing blow to the warden's head, and as he stumbled backward, Green unloaded a blast from the shotgun, striking the warden's left arm and propelling him into the ditch.

Believing they had just killed the warden, Green, Thayer, Durrill and Curtis had just began loading into the car when they spotted the warden's sedan coming over the hill. Pausing for a few seconds, the inmates raised their weapons as the sedan came to an abrupt stop. Inside the warden's car were Deputy Warden J.D. Galvin, Officer I.W. Mooney, Officer Ray Alexander and W.S. Bradford, mayor of nearby McClouth, Kansas. One of the inmates opened fire on the group. Officer Mooney was shot through the neck and left forearm. Deputy Warden Galvin and Bradford were both injured by flying glass. Galvin was cut below the right eye and on the left side of his head, and Bradford's left cheek was cut. Officer Alexander, who was in the backseat, emerged from the car and opened fire with a Thompson submachine gun. Realizing there was no danger to the warden or any other hostage, the posse members opened fire on the four inmates, using shotguns loaded with buckshot. Deputy Sheriff Jimmy Irwin also opened up with a Thompson submachine gun, and Officer Harry DeVeau, who was the officer on horseback, fired on the car with a pistol. Officer Mooney's injuries were the worst, and the sedan stopped at a nearby farmhouse, where the posse dressed his wounds and called for an ambulance.

The getaway car was struck by gunfire numerous times, inflicting serious damage to the windshield and radiator. As the inmates piled into the car, volley after volley of bullets rained down from all directions. Green, who was at the wheel, was struck in the head by a bullet; temporarily blinded, he struck the officer's horse that had been left beside the road, breaking its legs. Green immediately turned into what he thought was a road only to find he had turned onto a muddy path leading toward another farmhouse. The car instantly became moored in the deep mud and stalled. Realizing there were more carloads of posse members advancing toward them on the road as well as a rather large group coming on foot across the fields, the inmates hunkered down alongside the coupe. Spying the nearby farmhouse, the four inmates made a mad dash. As they approached the house, Earl Thayer, the oldest of the escapees at age sixty-three, advised the others it wasn't wise to enter the house, preferring to continue their flight in the open. "We have a one-in-a-million chance of escape if we enter that house," said Thayer. Curtis replied, "We'll never be taken alive!" Fearing Curtis's reply, Thayer called out, "Then if you don't think I'm leaving you in a lurch, I'll go on alone." Curtis replied, "Go to it, but we're staying here."

Seventy-three-year-old Emerson Salisbury, the only occupant of the isolated farmhouse, saw the five men running toward him. Stepping on to the porch, the farmer called out, "Howdy boys, you going hunting?" The immediate reply was, "No, were being hunted; we're gonna rest awhile, and we're doing it in your house." As the inmates forced Salisbury back into his house, one of them asked, "You got any guns?" As Salisbury replied, one of the inmates escorted him into another room, where he retrieved an old double-barreled shotgun. As Salisbury removed the shells from the weapon, the inmate laughed and said, "We don't want that; we've got plenty of guns." As confusion and desperation mounted, Thayer continued through the house and out a back window.

As the inmate and the farmer made their way back to the front room, the house was suddenly besieged by gunfire from all directions. Salisbury exclaimed, "What are they doing shooting at the house?" One of the inmates replied, "No, that's just a signal—they won't start blasting for a while." As the posse began increasing in numbers around the Salisbury home, the men outside took up positions behind trees, woodpiles and outbuildings. Soldiers set up machine guns, and soon the command came from across the yard: "Give yourselves up!" This was met with a hail of bullets from inside the house. For the next two hours, the two-story farm house resembled a battlefield.

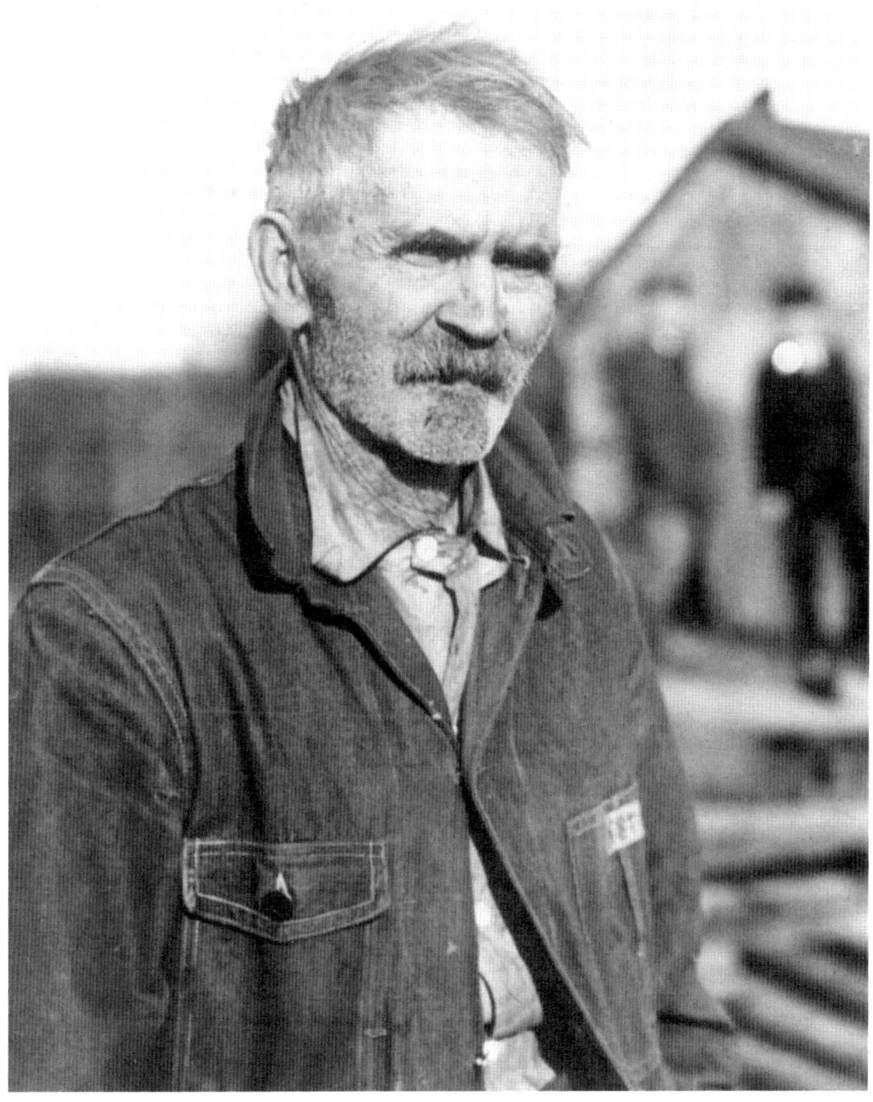

Seventy-three-year-old Emerson Salisbury commented to the media, "There was so much tear gas I thought I was gonna suffocate." *Courtesy of the author.*

A crowd of curious onlookers began to gather along Highway 92. General Heintzleman directed a couple of soldiers to hold the onlookers back at a safe distance. The Bell School House was located upon a hill directly across the road from the Salisbury farm. At this point, it was approximately 12:30 p.m., and the school was full of students. As the

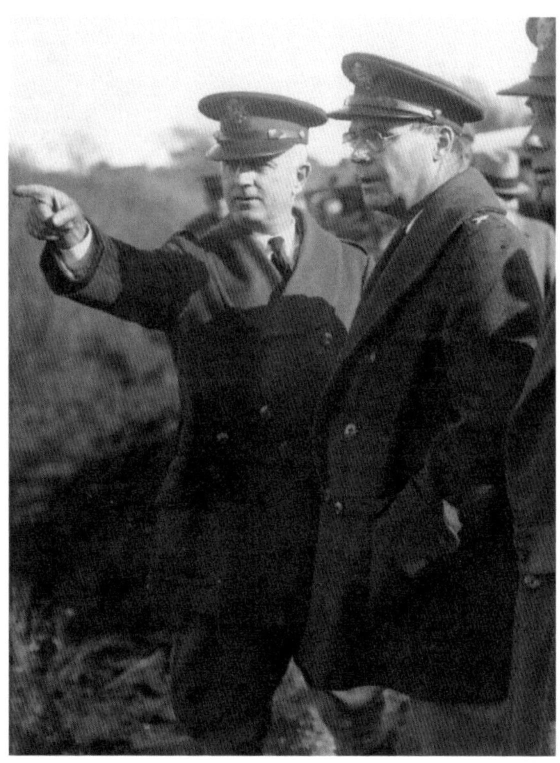

Major General Stuart Heintzleman receiving an update from a staff officer. *Courtesy of the author.*

shooting intensified, the school was hit by stray bullets. Several of the prison officers began evacuating the students, taking them to the south and out of harm's way. As more posse members arrived, Deputy Warden Galvin gave orders to circle the house. Two Leavenworth car salesmen, Tim Sherman and James Cobb, came across Warden White, who was being tended to by a couple of soldiers. They loaded him into their car and headed back toward town and Cushing Hospital.

As the shoot-out was underway at the Salisbury home, Berta, Brown and Underwood were making their way across fields by walking through ravines and overgrown woods. At the farm of C.V. Brady, they were unable to find a car, so they stole a plow horse and a saddle horse. As they lit out, both animals began to buck and threw all three men to the ground. Back on foot, the trio was spotted by army planes in a ravine along Highway 92 on the Dietrich farm. The planes began circling the area, which alerted the soldiers and prison officers. Arriving shortly thereafter, the posse found the three inmates attempting to hide in a hollow under some brush. Leading the posse was army captain E.A. Keck, who called out, "Put 'em up or we'll shoot!" As the three stood up, Brown was heard telling the other two, "We haven't a chance." As he pulled a stick of dynamite from his coat, Brown remarked, "We all might as well go up to see St. Peter." After striking a match, he was unable to light the fuse because it was wet. A volley of shots immediately rang out, two of which struck Berta. Zerbst ordered the trio out of the hollow, and as they were making their way up the hill, Berta fell backwards. Underwood and Brown were then ordered to carry Berta up the hill. The three had in their possession three shotguns, two dynamite bombs and a bottle of nitroglycerin. All three were swiftly returned to the institution, where Brown and Underwood were placed in solitary confinement and Berta was placed in the institution's hospital. As Underwood was hurriedly placed inside a cell in solitary, he removed a half-stick of dynamite from his jacket pocket. Handing it to Lieutenant John C. Krautz, Underwood stated, "I won't have any use for this anymore; I don't understand how this wasn't found—I have been searched three different times." The bomb still had the cap and fuse intact and was found to have eight penny nails taped around the outside.

With three of the escapees captured, the remaining officers, soldiers and other members of the posse headed to the Salisbury home. As they took up positions with the others, the gun battled intensified. For the next three hours, bullets fired from all directions were met with bullets shot from inside the house. Tear gas was thrown into the home in an attempt to smoke out the malefactors. At one point, the three inmates were holed up on the second floor with their hostage. Salisbury was able to slip away from his captors and climbed into the attic. His attempt to wave a white handkerchief from a window was met by several rounds fired in his direction. Once those on the ground realized he was the hostage, they were able to coax him out of the attic. Swinging the attic door open, Salisbury was able to run down the stairs and out the front door. A loud cheer erupted as the elder Salisbury was met by his son and rushed toward cover.

At approximately 3:00 p.m., there was a lull in the gun battle. Several minutes passed without a shot being fired. Suddenly, Fritz Walkenbach, armed with a .45-caliber pistol in each hand, stormed the front door. Gaining entry and followed by other members of the posse, Walkenbach made his way to the second floor. There, he found the three inmates huddled together in a pool of blood. Also found were three shotguns, a rifle, two revolvers and several boxes of shells.[39]

For the next few hours, as the local posse and curious onlookers retreated to their homes, local police, sheriff's deputies and prison officers searched

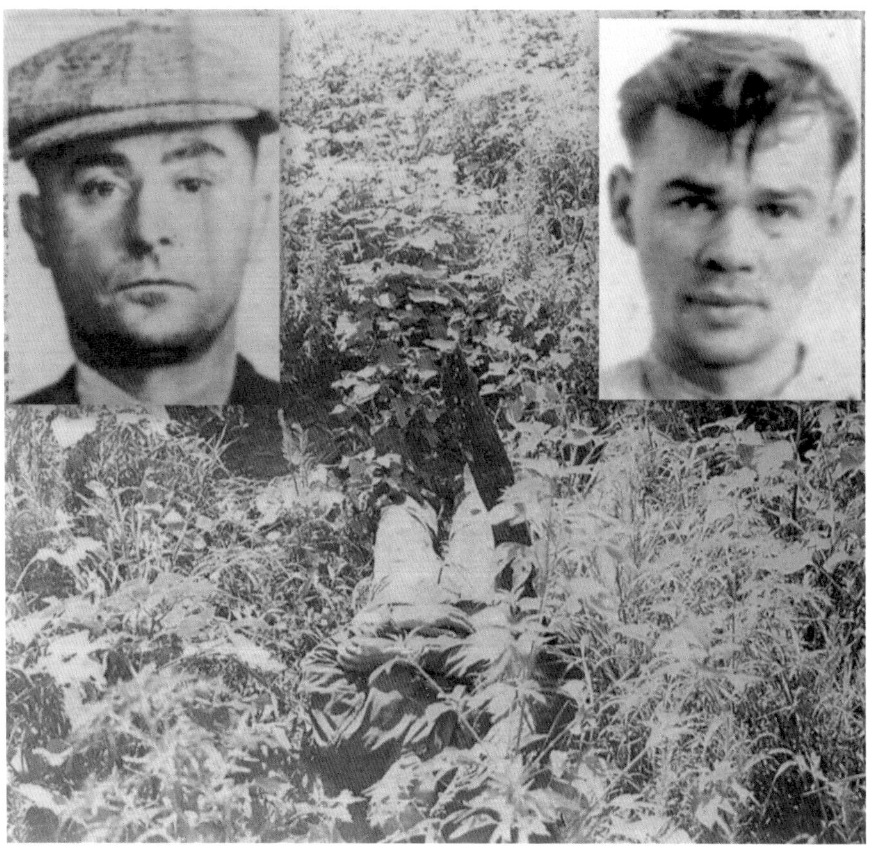

Tom Underwood (*left*), Stanley Brown (*right*) and Charlie Berta laying in a ravine shortly after capture. All were returned to the institution. Upon being placed in solitary confinement, Underwood pulled a stick of dynamite from his coat, saying, "I won't have any use for this anymore." *Courtesy of the author.*

the countryside until dark on the hunt for the last of the escapees, Earl Thayer. Dawn broke on Saturday, December 12, and the search began again, led by local law enforcement officers. Still, the officers were unable to find the sixty-three-year-old Oklahoma outlaw before sundown. At approximately 2:30 p.m. on Monday, December 14, J.F. Masterson and his buddy Roy Dougherty had just put on a pot of coffee inside Masterson's garage at the corner of Twentieth and Spruce Streets. Strolling through the door came a beleaguered man carrying a rifle. The wet, tired and hungry Thayer offered his rifle in exchange for a cup of coffee. After taking the rifle, Masterson handed it to Dougherty, who immediately drew down on the old

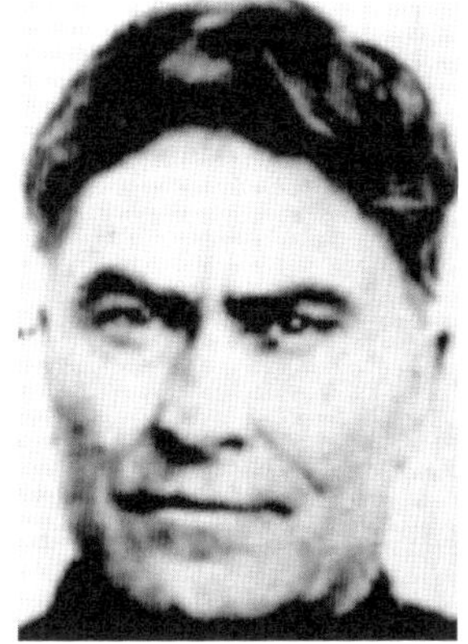

Left: Earl Thayer avoided capture for two days by using skills he had learned during his days as an Oklahoma outlaw. *Courtesy of the author.*

Below: Earl Thayer, tired and sick, entered a garage located at the corner of Twentieth and Spruce Streets and owned by J.F. Masterson (*left*). Thayer traded his rifle for a cup of coffee and patiently waited as Masterson called authorities and Roy Dougherty (*right*) covered him with the rifle. *Courtesy of the author.*

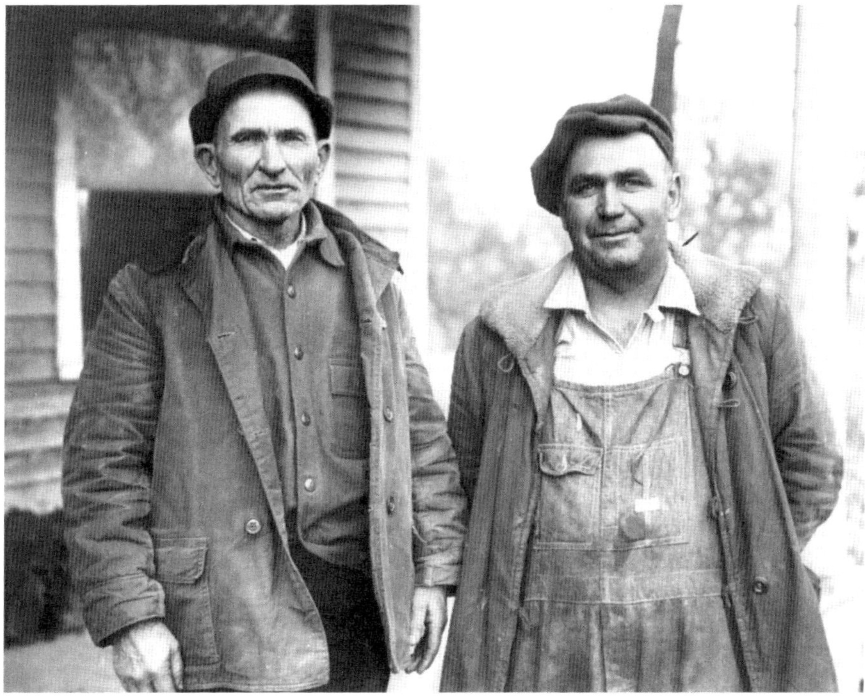

convict, who offered no resistance. Deputy Sheriff Roy Murray arrived to find Thayer waiting patiently and drinking his coffee. Upon his return to the institution, Thayer was placed in the institution's hospital and diagnosed with pneumonia, exhaustion and dehydration. During his examination by doctors, Thayer commented, "Well, I didn't do so bad for an old man."[40]

8

DAMN SNITCHES

As the events unfolded on Friday, December 11, 1931, chaos ruled the institution. Rumors added to the discontent amongst the prisoners, who could be heard cursing and shouting while they were locked inside their cells. A chorus of "every day will be Sunday bye and bye" rang throughout the institution. The one constant rumor relayed to staff was that Curtis, Durrill and Green had been captured and subsequently murdered by officers. So strong was this rumor that inmates working the powerhouse staged a strike on December 15, refusing to work and singing "we won't be home until morning" as they tossed chunks of coal over a fence. Over the next few days, officers were able to restore order at the facility. Inmates remained in their cells throughout the weekend and into the following week.

During the weekend and into Monday, investigators and the institution's executive staff conducted meetings at which the institutional records of each of the escapees were reviewed. Links between the inmates were reviewed in earnest—where they worked, with whom they corresponded and associated and their cellmates. During this part of the investigation, it was noticed that Durrill, Thayer and Curtis were all members of the same gang and had all been received at Leavenworth together on the same day after their sentencings.

During the evening of December 18, officers conducted a mass shakedown of the institution. Particular attention was paid to the job sites of each of the escapees. In the electrical shop, letters were found stuffed into the cubbyhole of a desk assigned to inmate William Tracy Stallings (No. 39246). Many of the letters had been received through the mail room, but one was of particular interest. The letter had been written that morning and was addressed to "Miss Bell West, Bristow, Oklahoma." In the letter, Stallings indicates that the letter would be going out by the "underground route" and asked that West send him six shirts (size thirty-eight) and six trunks (size thirty-two). He also relayed that he would like to have four shirts (size thirty-eight) and four trunks (size forty-two) sent as a present to the individual helping get the letters out and the clothes in. The letter indicated the ease with which the letters and packages could be sent and received. His instructions indicated that the clothes were to be sent to the following address: H.C. Burdgess, 602 Spruce Street, Leavenworth, Kansas. Burdgess was the chief engineer of the institution. The desk of Stallings also contained a set of keys that opened tool cabinets and lockers throughout all of the shop areas.

As the mass shakedown of the institution came to a close, investigators turned to interviewing all of the inmates inside the facility. These types of investigations are usually conducted in each individual cell house. Inmates

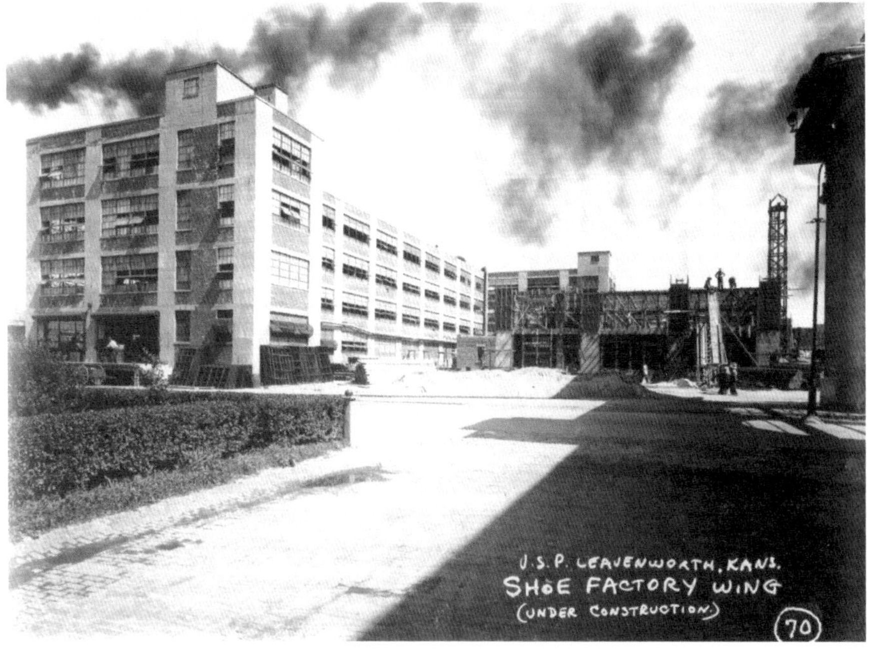

Federal Prison Industries building showing east wing under construction. To the right are the east gate towers. It was through the east gate that the weapons entered the prison, were unloaded at the dock to the left and were wheeled to the oil house in the center. *Courtesy of the author.*

are generally escorted one by one from their cells by officers, placed in a closed office and asked a series of questions. Most inmates will simply state they know nothing, and they are then returned to their cells. During these interviews on December 12, FBI agents Hugh Larimer and F.J. Lackey interviewed two inmates who claimed to have inside knowledge of the escape plan and all who participated. In a summary report dated February 5, 1932, and written by agents Lackey, Larimer and R.G. Harvey, the agents identified these inmates as confidential informants (CIs) No. 1 and No. 2.

As the interview got underway with CI No. 1, the informant advised Larimer that Stanley Brown had attempted an escape from the institution in October 1930 for which he had served a stretch in segregation and suffered a reduction in grade. On or about February 3, 1931, Brown was approached by another inmate, Moe Raskin, who told him of a plan to smuggle firearms into the prison and how those weapons could be used during another escape.

Raskin was able to observe any and all shipments that entered the institution through the east gate and how they were handled once they made their way to the factory delivery dock. Shipments from the G.R. Cummings Jr. and Company and Hadley Bros. of St. Louis, Missouri, contained materials such as glue, oil and shoe paste. A standing order from the factory manager made it clear that shipments such as these were not to be opened or inspected because doing so caused the materials to dry out and become unusable.

Raskin turned his attention to whether or not Brown was interested and if he had outside contacts that could provide money and a getaway car on the day of the escape. Brown assured Raskin that money and a car would not be a problem, but he wanted to take some time to think about the plan and talk it over with another inmate, Harry Sullivan. Sullivan had long been a friend of Brown's and had, in fact, been his coconspirator in his previous escape. Both men had attempted to dig their way under the prison wall. That plan fell apart when they discovered that the rumors of the wall extending forty feet below the surface as well as forty feet above the surface turned out to be true. Complicating the matter further, Brown and Sullivan had been discovered missing, and instead of surrendering, they decided to wait it out and hide underground until the search for them had been called off, thinking that they could then climb over the wall under cover of night. That plan literally became a wash after a few days of constant rain. The October rains had softened the ground, and an officer making rounds on the compound discovered the pair when he happened over a spot that gave way, causing the two would-be escapees to appear.

After conferring with Sullivan, Brown again spoke with Raskin and assured him that he could raise between $300 and $500. Brown asked Raskin whether he knew of any outside parties who could provide aid in the escape, and Raskin agreed that he would see what could be arraigned. Raskin also told Brown that he was considering including inmates John Kulick, Harry Sullivan and "Old Fogey" Woods in the escape. Brown's curiosity made him ask why Raskin would help Kulick and Woods. To ensure loyalty, Raskin had asked the others to take part in the murder of an inmate identified as Dago George. Brown voiced his disagreement with this show of loyalty and refused to take part, but Kulick and Woods assured Raskin they would "bump" Dago George because Raskin was entitled to that much consideration, since Dago George was no good anyway.

A few days passed, and Raskin approached Brown with the news that he could provide the outside help but had decided against taking an active part in the escape. This sudden change in plans raised the suspicions of Brown and Sullivan, and they decided to avoid Raskin from that point forward. During this time, Sullivan had received word that his father had enlisted a substantial amount of cooperation on the outside, and it appeared that he (Sullivan) was about to obtain his release by way of a commuted sentence.

Wise to a possible double cross from Raskin, Brown and Sullivan continued to discuss the plan on their own. One of the possibilities involved using an individual who was about to be released. This individual would, upon release, make contact with the outside help to discuss the plan and put it in motion. A short time afterward, Brown approached inmate George Curtis, and much to his surprise, Curtis was working on a similar plan. Curtis assured Brown that his plan was much better and that he had already thoroughly investigated his plan and determined that there was no chance of a slipup. A visit had already been set up by Curtis to discuss whether the route for smuggling "a package" into the institution was good and that this "route" had been previously used by escaped inmate Frank Nash. Curtis explained that Nash had recently used "the route" to send a package to an unidentified inmate and that said package contained $200 in cash. The test was to see if the package would be delivered to the inmate without being opened. Curtis assured Brown that the test was an overwhelming success and that he himself was going to use the same system of smuggling.

The informant continued, providing information about an unidentified woman who had visited with Curtis in March 1931. During that visit, the woman disclosed that she was there for the benefit of Frank Nash and was to ascertain whether Curtis wanted stuff (presumed to be firearms) sent into the prison using the same method as the previous package. Curtis initially said yes but soon changed his mind. As the visit continued, the woman told Curtis that Nash's plan called for five men to come up the main drive of the prison in one Lincoln and one Cadillac. These men would be armed with machine guns and would draw down on the front tower officers with instructions to fire only if they met resistance. The woman also assured Curtis that the local highways had been run by Nash himself and the escape route had been perfected. After the visit, Curtis had approached Brown with details of the visit and was upset with himself that he had forgotten to tell the woman to advise Nash that the "route" would be the method used to smuggle the weapons into the institution.

In late May or early June, the unidentified woman again visited Curtis at the institution. She first apologized for not visiting sooner, explaining that the killing of a Notre Dame student near Webb City, Missouri, had interfered with her ability to make contact with Nash. She then advised Curtis that Nash and his associates were ready to proceed and asked if the same method of introduction should be used. Without going into detail, Curtis told her no and made no definite plans with her.

Shortly after that visit, Curtis sent out a letter on the underground route addressed to an unidentified employee or guest of either the St. Paul Hotel or the Ryan Hotel in St. Paul, Minnesota. The letter in question was known to have been sent out of the penitentiary using an unidentified contact in the inmate library. A few months had passed when Curtis approached Brown, telling him that the escape plan and smuggling of contraband had been delayed by the killing of Harry "Slim Jones" Morris near Red Wing, Minnesota. Morris, a known bank robber, had been an associate of Frank Weber and Leavenworth inmate Tom Underwood.

Prior to the fallout between inmates Raskin, Brown and Sullivan, both Brown and Sullivan had agreed to use a soon-to-be-released inmate by the name of Harold Fontaine as the outside man. Neither had ever disclosed the name of Fontaine to Raskin due in part to their mistrust of Raskin and fear of a double cross. The two had never even disclosed the name of the individual to George Curtis. In fact, the two had not approached Fontaine until a couple of weeks prior to his November 6 release. Curtis approached Fontaine first and disclosed the plan of shipping weapons into the penitentiary shoe factory by hiding them in a barrel of shoe paste that could be procured from the G.R. Cummings Jr. and Company in St. Louis. Fontaine became extremely interested and was soon introduced to Kulick and Brown. As the three filled in Fontaine about the details of the plan, they agreed that no one was to provide any details to Raskin. Fontaine agreed to be the outside man and provided Curtis with his home address in Windsor, Canada.

On the evening of November 5, Curtis approached Fontaine and told him that word had come from Nash and that the outside plans were lined up and ready to go. The next morning, Fontaine was released from the penitentiary and made his way to the local train station, where he boarded a train headed home. A few short hours after Fontaine's release, Curtis wrote Fontaine a letter and had it mailed out through the underground source. Fontaine was provided with twenty-five dollars in cash for expenses and given instructions to telegraph Curtis upon receipt of the letter. Further, he was instructed to lay low for a few days and then take a train to Cicero, Illinois. Once there, he was to proceed to the Annetta Hotel and make contact with Nash. On the evening of November 13, Curtis received the following telegram: "Mother and Frances are well I will leave next week Love—Margaret M. Brown."

CI No. 1 explained that the word "Mother" was a reference to Fontaine, and "Frances" was a reference to Nash. All indications from that telegram made it clear that the plan was underway to procure the weapons and barrel of shoe paste and ship them into Leavenworth. Plans began on the inside. Kulick was assigned to the oil house, which placed him in charge of the shoe factory supplies, and his duties included advising when those supplies needed to be ordered. Kulick requested an order of shoe paste through the shoe factory office on December 4, and the order went through to G.R. Cummings Jr. and Company that same day.

On December 5, inmate Stanley Brown received the following telegram that Fontaine sent from East St. Louis, Illinois: "Aunt Emma very ill leaving St. Louis tonight—Margerette M Brown."

This telegram indicated to the escapees that the shipment of contraband had been shipped and was indeed arriving in a barrel of shoe paste.

The interview with CI No. 2 uncovered much of the same information but provided investigators with additional details. CI No. 2 stated that in late June or early July, George Curtis approached inmate Tom Underwood with the details of the escape and inquired if he wanted "in." Underwood accepted the offer without hesitation. Curtis confided the details of how the weapons were to be smuggled inside the institution. Curtis also told Underwood that there were other unnamed parties aware of the escape and that contact with those on the outside was made possible by an officer working in the shoe factory. This unnamed officer was carrying letters in and out of the institution and was charging a dollar per letter each way. CI No.

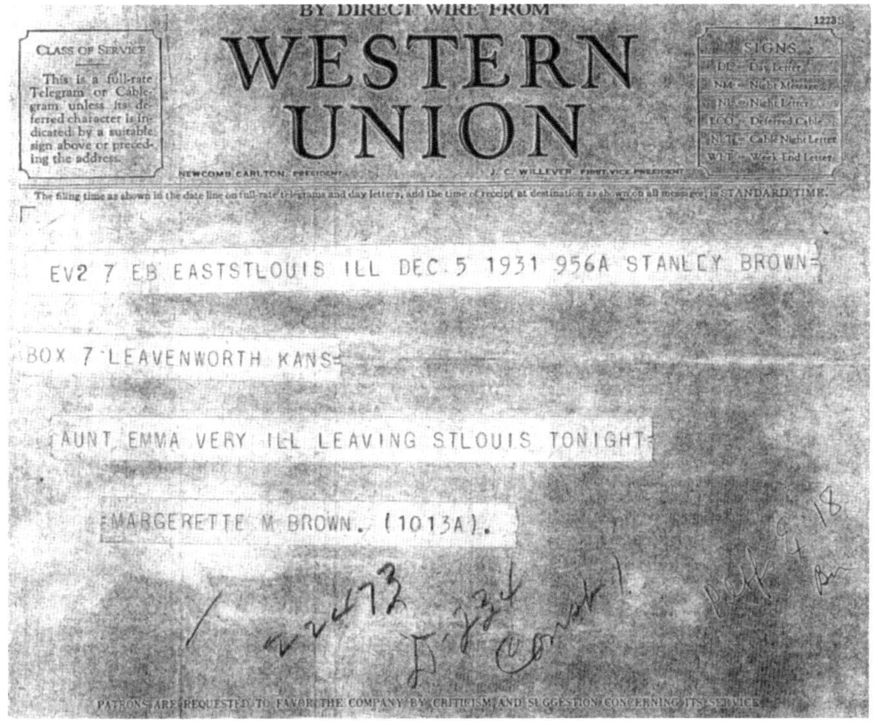

BY DIRECT WIRE FROM

WESTERN UNION

CLASS OF SERVICE

This is a full-rate Telegram or Cablegram unless its deferred character is indicated by a suitable sign above or preceding the address.

SIGNS

DL = Day Letter
NM = Night Message
NL = Night Letter
LCO = Deferred Cable
NLT = Cable Night Letter
WLT = Week End Letter

NEWCOMB CARLTON, PRESIDENT — J. C. WILLEVER, FIRST VICE PRESIDENT

The filing time as shown in the date line on full-rate telegrams and day letters, and the time of receipt at destination as shown on all messages, is STANDARD TIME.

EV2 7 EB EASTSTLOUIS ILL DEC 5 1931 956A STANLEY BROWN=

BOX 7 LEAVENWORTH KANS=

AUNT EMMA VERY ILL LEAVING STLOUIS TONIGHT=

MARGERETTE M BROWN. (1013A).

PATRONS ARE REQUESTED TO FAVOR THE COMPANY BY CRITICISM AND SUGGESTION CONCERNING ITS SERVICE

Telegram sent to inmate Stanley Brown advising, "Aunt Emma very ill leaving St. Louis tonight," which confirmed that the weapons were on their way. *Courtesy of the author.*

2 also divulged the name of Frank Nash as the outside man setting up the purchase of the contraband and that at least seven guns had been ordered.

In late November, CI No. 2 alleged that Curtis again approached Underwood, advising him that the plan may have to be abandoned. Curtis had become aware that things had gotten "hot" for Nash and that he was doing quite a bit of "jumping around." This was also the first time the informant had heard Thomas Holden and Francis Keating mentioned as the men working with Nash. The other name mentioned, "Monk," was unknown to the informant. The only information the informant provided was that "Monk" had recently been released after doing a six-year stretch out of Detroit and that he was the former cellmate of an inmate named "Red" Ryan.

Both informants told investigators that on December 8, around 2:00 p.m., the barrel containing the weapons entered the east gate and was delivered to the shoe factory dock. Both reported that Officer Haag had sent inmate John Lee Jackson to the oil house with instructions for inmate John Kulick to come and get the barrel of shoe paste. Once Kulick had taken the barrel back to the oil house, it took approximately thirty minutes for it to be unpacked.

Inside the barrel were six guns, seventeen sticks of dynamite, a box containing one hundred blasting caps and approximately one hundred feet of fuse. A letter was supposed to have accompanied the weapons, but one was not found. It was also divulged that around 4:00 p.m. that same day, Underwood met with inmate Will Green on the second tier of B cell house, where both inmates entered the cell occupied by Green. Green reportedly removed a .32-20–caliber revolver from his jacket pocket to show Underwood and assured him that the other weapons had arrived. It was also alleged that on the afternoon of December 10, the officer in D cell house had almost busted Curtis, who had been cooking nitroglycerin inside his cell when the fumes became overwhelming.

Investigators now had a large piece of the puzzle that provided them not only with answers about how the weapons made it into the institution but the names of at least four outside accomplices. Armed with the above information, the agents decided it was time to interview all of the staff members and inmates who would have come in contact with the barrel of shoe paste.

Before those interviews were conducted, FBI agents Larimer and Lackey took the opportunity to visit the various railroad offices located in downtown Leavenworth. While at the Missouri Pacific Railroad office, it was discovered that a half barrel of shoe paste was received, consigned from G.R. Cummings Jr. and Company in St. Louis, Missouri, to the U.S. Penitentiary Leavenworth on Missouri Pacific waybill No. 27267, dated September 5, 1931. Records further indicated that the half barrel of shoe paste was signed for and picked up by Officer I.W. Mooney on December 8, 1931. During his interview, Officer Mooney remembered delivering a red half barrel to the institution that day and stated that he had left the barrel on the shoe factory dock and turned over the freight bill to Officer Haag.

Upon returning to the institution, Larimer and Lackey conferred with O.N. Shelton, the business manager of the prison industries. It was Shelton's job to order and receive into inventory all supplies needed for the factory. After conducting a thorough check of his records, the agents found nothing that indicated an order being placed or received on December 8, 1931, in reference to waybill No. 27267. It was noted that an order was placed on December 4 for a half barrel of shoe paste and three cans of leather dressing that were received on December 9 on Missouri Pacific waybill No. 30079. Shelton advised agents that in each instance, all items received by the

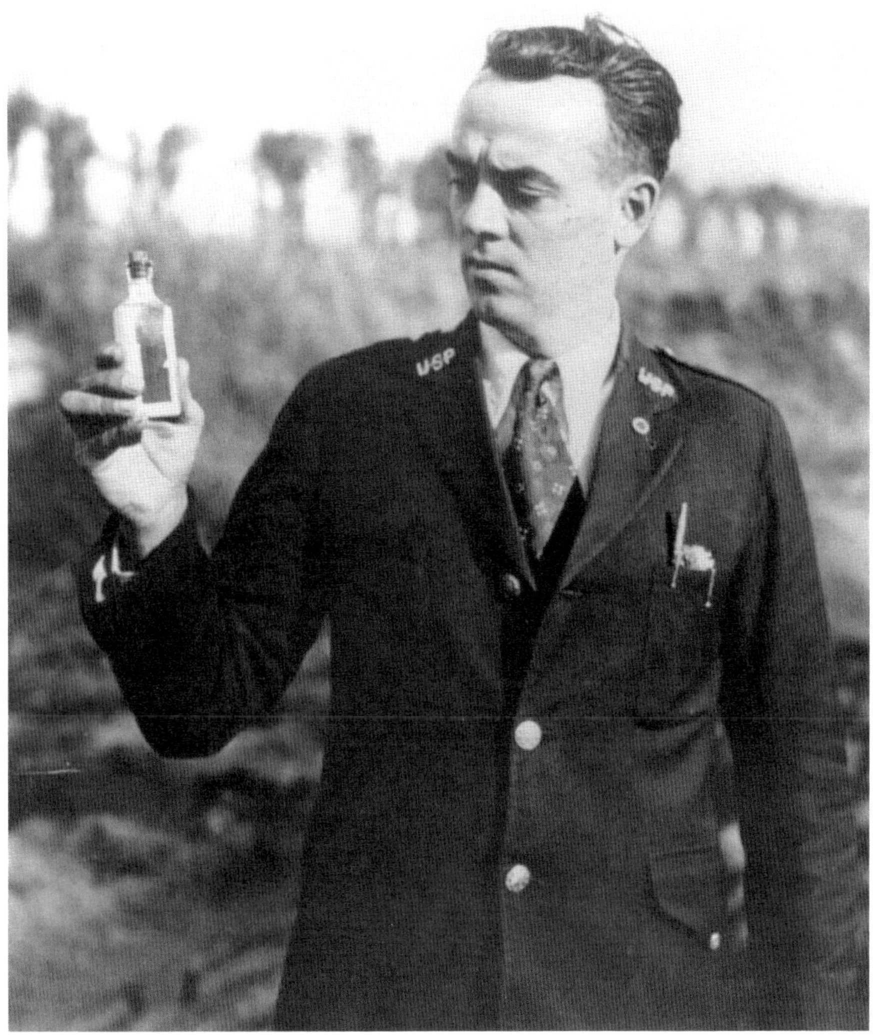

Officer C.D. Wood displays a bottle of nitroglycerin found on one of the captured inmates. *Courtesy of the author.*

factory, along with all documentation, were received by Officer Haag. Haag would then turn over all freight bills and other documentation to Shelton's inmate secretary, William Tebo Shafer.

In a detailed report written on December 20, 1931, by Special Agent in Charge Gus T. Jones and given to FBI director J. Edgar Hoover, it was disclosed that on the evening of December 18, another CI had provided information through an unidentified officer to Acting Warden Fred Zerbst. The informant was interviewed that evening by Agents Larimer and Lackey, who describe the individual as a first-time inmate who knew nothing of the "convict code." The informant is assigned to the third floor of the factory, where his job is inspecting shoes. His desk is just outside the first-aid room, where inmate George Curtis was assigned. The CI stated that on the afternoon of December 10, he was standing near a window between 2:30 and 3:00 p.m. and observed an unidentified officer enter the first-aid room. The informant advised that the officer hurriedly removed two pistols from his rear pockets, handing them to inmate Curtis, and as Curtis was placing them in a drawer, the officer pulled two more pistols from under his coat (from his waistband), handing them to Curtis, who hurriedly placed them in a drawer. The inmate advised that he didn't think much of the incident until the day of the escape but was hesitant to say anything because he did not know the name of the officer. During the morning of December 18, the officer was seen talking with inmate Ed Slayton (No. 37393), and the informant later asked about the officer's name. Slayton gave the officer's name as C.A. Carlson.

As of the writing of this report, agents conferred with Warden Zerbst and it was decided to handle this part of the investigation in a discreet manner. Everyone was in agreement that more time was needed to build a case against Carlson. It was also agreed that the letter written by inmate Stallings addressed to Miss Bell West was to be photocopied and mailed. A mail cover was placed on the home of H.C. Burdgess with instructions that any package received from Miss West or bearing the postmark of Bristow, Oklahoma, be immediately reported to the agents. After inspection, it would be delivered, and Carlson would be observed as he entered the institution.

The following information was obtained during an interview with inmate Kenneth Frye (No. 37141), the secretary of industries assistant superintendent Collins. Frye relayed to the agents that his office is just off the small stairwell on the southeast corner of the shoe factory and opposite the first-aid room. On the morning of December 11, he witnessed inmate Thayer in the first-aid room at about 8:30 a.m. talking to Curtis but did not see any guns at that time. As he passed through the small stairwell, he noticed inmate Will Green engaged in a confidential conversation with Officer Leo Aaron and overheard Green comment, "If anything goes wrong, it won't be your fault." Not less than fifteen minutes later, he observed Officer Aaron intently staring out the window toward the main building of the institution, and at that time, he could see officers running toward the rear corridor and knew the escape was taking place.[41]

9

OUTSIDE IN

From the moment the last shots were fired at the Emerson Salisbury home, chaos reigned. Unlike at today's crime scenes, where the area is cordoned off and evidence is preserved and collected, a mad rush of curious onlookers, posse members and officers milled about the area. In a tape-recorded narrative from years later, Rose Haas Frietchen, one of the inmates' hostages who had been left behind by the escapees at the Joe Gates farm, recalled being amongst a group of onlookers standing along Highway 92.[42] Shortly after the shoot-out ended, she was amongst the first group to make its way up to the Salisbury home. Rose recalled that the house was a mess and there was an overwhelming smell of tear gas. "It's a two-story house, and there was blood on the stairs, blood everywhere." As people milled about the house, they began tearing away at everything they could take as a souvenir. As they brought the inmates' bodies down the stairs, Rose recalled, "Their heads bounced off of each step, and they were thrown out on the porch." Pausing for a few seconds, she says, "Well, I can see their bodies lay there yet."

Since they arrived at the scene shortly after the shooting began, FBI agents F.J. Lackey and Hugh Larimer were engaged in the shoot-out. They were at the rear of the home when entry was made by Fritz Walkenbach, followed by other posse members, and were amongst the first to enter the second-floor room where the inmates' bodies were found. In his official report, local mortician Ted Sexton indicated that Curtis and Durrill had been shot in the head and that Green died of a self-inflicted gunshot to the right temple.

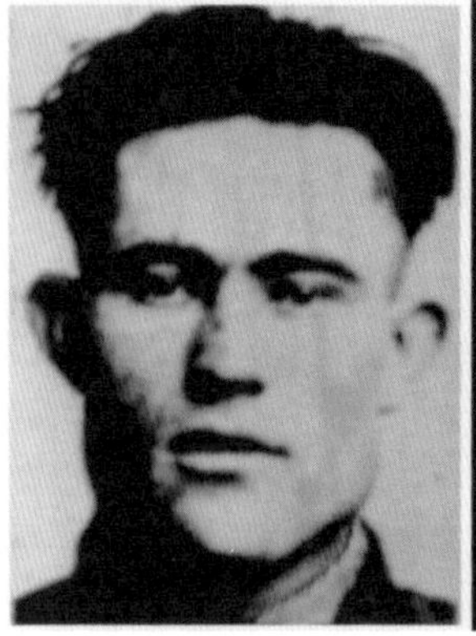
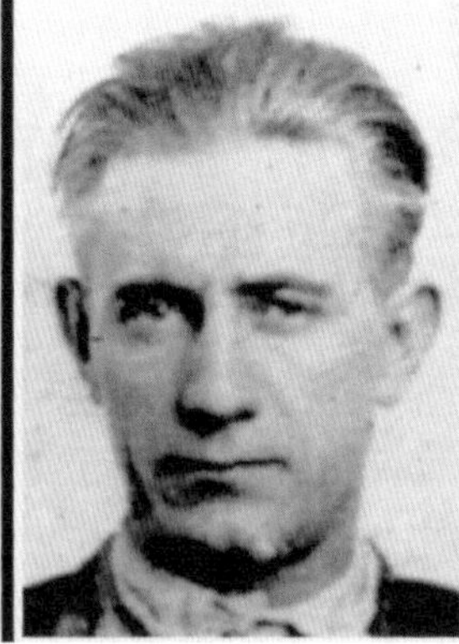
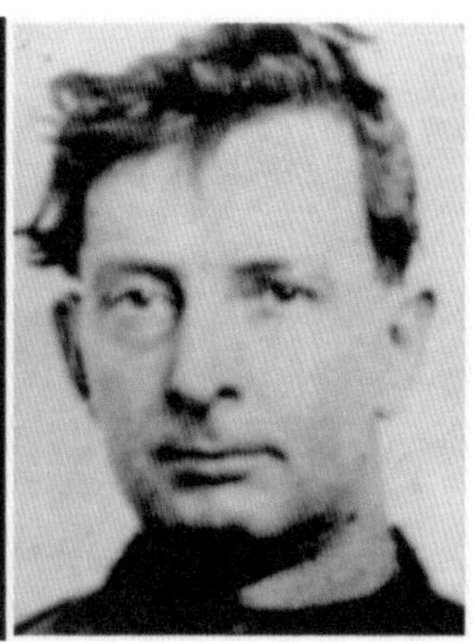

The official death records signed by Ted Sexton indicate Will "Boxcar" Green, George "Whitey" Curtis and Grover C. Durrill all died from self-inflicted gunshots to the head. During the investigation, it was uncovered that at least six of the seven escapees had made a suicide pact to avoid being returned to the institution. *Courtesy of the author.*

Further hindering the investigation was the fact that all the weapons the escapees had in their possession during the shoot-out had been picked up, and the agents found it impossible to ascertain which weapon each of the inmates possessed because those involved in the manhunt were milling about the house, and all were in possession of guns.[43]

Upon their return to the institution, the agents asked Acting Warden Zerbst to conduct a check of all officers to see if any of them had any of the weapons found on the inmates. Officer Joseph Concanon turned in a .38-caliber Smith and Wesson pistol and indicated that he had found it under the body of Curtis. A .32-20–caliber Colt pistol removed from the hand of Green was given to the agents by Officer E.M. Taylor. Agent Lackey had also recovered a .38-caliber revolver from Roy Schollars, a local resident who had taken it as a souvenir. A .38-caliber pistol and 20-gauge shotgun recovered by army captain E.A. Keck were turned in to the Leavenworth armory. At the time he was apprehended, inmate Thayer was in possession of a Winchester .30-30 carbine rifle with a twenty-inch barrel.

Armed with the information received from the confidential informants (CIs) during the interview process and the serial numbers of the weapons smuggled into Leavenworth, agents went to work tying those weapons to those believed to be outside conspirators. By December 16, all of the weapons manufacturers had been supplied with the serial numbers, and an exhaustive search of their records had been conducted. The four pistols had originally been sold to sporting goods and hardware stores in San Francisco,

Fort Worth, Peoria and Chicago. The Winchester was originally sold as part of an order received by the State of Indiana and issued to the National Guard. The Ithaca Auto & Burglar 20-gauge shotgun was originally sold to the Buckeye Cycle Company in Akron, Ohio. Agents in those areas checked with each company as to the sale of those weapons and began interviewing the original owners.

Records at the Buckeye Cycle Company failed to indicate whether the weapon had ever been received or sold. Employees were interviewed, and each remembered having a similar shotgun in stock but couldn't recall if it had been sold or sent back to the factory. Agent J.E. Fitzpatrick followed up with the Ithaca Gun Company and requested additional information concerning the Auto & Burglar shotgun. Records indicated that the weapon had shipped to the Buckeye Cycle Company on March 30, 1925, and was returned and received back at Ithaca on May 14, 1925. Records further indicated that the shotgun was shipped that same day to Hibbard Spencer Bartlett Hardware Company in Chicago.

In a memo written by Special Agent A.D. Mehegan of the Cincinnati field office, it was indicated that L.A. Pennypacker, of the Indiana adjutant general's office, contacted him and advised that National Guard storekeeper Charles Long had been in service for a long period of time and could possibly help with questions concerning the Winchester .30-30 rifle. Agent Mehegan followed up with Long, who indicated that the state had purchased five hundred of those particular rifles in November 1917. They were placed into inventory to replace weapons that were used in the war. In 1920, the rifles were ordered to be sold, and he recalled three hundred of them being sold to a William R. Burkhard believed to be in Denver, Colorado. The remainder were individually sold, and a fire in 1928 destroyed those records. He also indicated that to his recollection, none of the serial numbers were ever recorded upon receipt or sale of those weapons.

As agents were following the trail of the weapons and explosives, another investigation was beginning that would tie together Frank Nash, Thomas James Holden, Francis Keating and Harold Fontaine as the outside conspirators. Information received during the inmate interviews named the Annetta Hotel in Cicero, Illinois, as the place Fontaine was to meet the others and put the plan into motion.

On January 14, 1932, Special Agent in Charge R.G. Harvey confided in a memo that he had contacted Agent McSwain at the Chicago field office to discuss options for investigating the Annetta Hotel. The hotel itself was located at 2417 South Fifty-Second Avenue in Cicero, which was the base of operations for Al Capone. Agents advised that many members of the Cicero Police Department were on Capone's payroll and that the hotel itself was known as a hangout for individuals of questionable character. Agents knew that if the time came to raid the Annetta Hotel, the local police would be of no assistance.

During a meeting with the Chicago field office, it was suggested to Harvey that he contact Alexander G. Jamie, the head of an organization known to the FBI as the Secret Six. Jamie, a former chief special agent of the Department of Justice and brother-in-law to Eliot Ness, led the group of six influential businessmen who aided in bringing down Capone. During the meeting, Jamie was supplied with pictures of Holden, Keating, Nash and Fontaine so his undercover agents could become familiar with their faces. It was advised that these agents should not carry these photographs or any other information with them. It was well known that the Cicero Police Department scrutinized all strangers checking into the Annetta.

Information obtained by agents calling on the offices of G.R. Cummings Jr. and Company in St. Louis, Missouri, disclosed that a man entered the company's offices between 10:00 and 11:00 a.m. on November 30, 1931. Witnesses advised that the man arrived and left in a yellow cab. The individual ordered one half barrel of number 10 Hub Doubler shoe paste and ordered it shipped to George H. Clark in Joliet, Illinois. Both the foreman, Theodore Heidinger, and the stenographer, Georgia Brandle, provided an accurate physical description of Harold Fontaine and identified him in a photograph.

On January 9, 1932, Special Agent in Charge (SAC) Quinn, at the St. Louis office, notified Special Agent Keating that a half barrel of Number 10 Hub Doubler shoe paste valued at eighteen dollars was consigned to a G.H. Clark of Joliet, Illinois, from G.R. Cummings Jr. and Company and shipped on waybill No. 2704 via the Chicago & Alton Railroad on November 30, 1931. SAC McSwain and Special Agent Keating conferred with Railway Express agents who found the records pertaining to this shipment. The barrel was delivered to the Joliet freight office on November 30 and handled by clerks John P. Murphy and Walter Miller. Upon arrival, the barrel was unloaded by freight employee Charles W. Skoien and placed in the freight room.

On the morning of December 3, two men entered the Joliet freight office. Clerks Murphy and Miller described the men as one being fairly tall and the other being short. Murphy indicated that the shorter of the two asked if a barrel of shoe paste had been delivered and gave the name of George Clark.

Murphy further stated that the man had noticed the barrel and stated, "Hey, that looks like our Barrel." The shipment was signed for by the man, and the fee of $5.97 was paid in cash. The barrel was then rolled out the door by both men. Agent Keating showed Murphy a photograph of Fontaine, and Murphy indicated that he was positive that was the man using the name George Clark. Agent Keating then showed Murphy a photograph of Frank Nash, and he positively identified him as the taller of the two men. Neither clerk identified photos of Holden or Keating. An analysis of the handwriting on the freight bill indicated that it was a positive match to known handwriting samples from Harold Fontaine provided by the prison.

On January 13, a confidential memo received at the Kansas City field office indicated that a check by Special Agents Mullen and Keating conducted on January 2 at the Western Union office in Chicago found that the telegram addressed to Stanley Brown that read, "Mother and Frances are well. I will leave next week, Love Margaret M. Brown," had been sent from the office located at 5205 Twenty-Fifth Street in Cicero, directly across the street from the Annetta Hotel. Handwriting analysis also showed that the telegram was written by Harold Fontaine.

On December 22, a report initiated by Special Agent D.W. Maher of the Kansas City field office indicated that exhaustive research into the weapons used in the escape had netted the following results: All of the manufacturers of the weapons held records that indicated that the weapons had been manufactured and sold between 1923 and 1925. The records of those sales indicated the original owners who had, in turn, sold them to various other individuals.

In a report filed by Special Agent in Charge Gus T. Jones on January 19, 1932, records of the Koran Jobbing Company in Peoria, Illinois, indicated that the Colt Army Special .38-caliber revolver with serial number 535071A had been sold on November 23, 1931, to a George D. Brighton, and on the same day, the Colt Police Special .38-caliber revolver with serial number 399560 had been sold to Jim Nelson. Also sold was a .30-30 Winchester rifle with the serial number 823576, a Smith and Wesson .38-caliber revolver with the serial number 136020, a Colt .32-20 revolver with the serial number defaced and one 20-gauge Auto & Burglar shotgun with the serial number 388712.

A follow-up interview was conducted with Louis A. Koran, owner of the Koran Jobbing Company. During the interview, Koran was shown photographs of Nash, Fontaine, Keating and Holden along with a photo of George Kelly. Also shown were photos of Earl Ogden, Phillip Stumpf and

William Penn. These three, along with Walter Schradrick, Leo Schradrick, James Julian and Hiram Miller, were Peoria residents who had been released from Leavenworth prior to the purchase of the firearms in question. Agents were convinced that Koran was evasive and hesitant to identify any one individual. His attention was directed to the pictures of Nash, Keating, Holden, Fontaine and Kelly, and his reply was, "Well, I'm certainly sorry, I am doing all I can to obtain some information about the fellows who did the purchasing, but I can't get any information about them, and I can't help what will be done."

In conferring with the Peoria chief of police, Charles A. Wilson, and chief of detectives, Fred Montgomery, agents learned that the only company in Peoria that handled dynamite, blasting caps and fuse would be the Dooley Brothers Company. A check with the company's stock clerk and shipping agent James K. Ganty produced very little. A check of company records dated November 1 through December 5, 1931, showed that not one sale had been made to anyone who had not purchased from the company for years.

As the investigation was advancing inside the institution, a couple of officers had stepped forward and confided in Acting Warden Zerbst and agreed to provide agents with statements on the condition that they could remain anonymous. The first officer stated that he had entered the officer's mess and observed Carlson in a close conversation with inmate R. LeCocq (No. 14938). The officer further related that Carlson appeared to be infuriated over the interruption and took LeCocq by the arm and began a conversation as Carlson and LeCocq walked away. This officer also stated that in early December 1931, at about 7:40 a.m., the inmate cook in hospital annex No. 1 had called out to Carlson, asking him if he wanted a cup of coffee, and Carlson had entered the kitchen, where he remained for an extended period of time. The inmate cook's name was Jack DePalma (No. 338361). The second, Officer Ernest R. Damon, whose name was not redacted from the FBI report, reported that on the morning of the escape, he was standing on the railroad track immediately north of hospital annex No. 1 and observed Carlson and Officer Leo Aaron walking in front of a double line of convicts. It is customary for one officer to lead and the other to walk beside the formation several feet from the front. Officer Damon stated that it was approximately 7:35 a.m. and that as they passed hospital annex No. 1, he observed Carlson nod his head twice as if signaling someone inside the building.

During the interview of Officer Leo Aaron, Agents Lackey and Larimer repeatedly asked if he had any knowledge of the impending escape or if he was associated in any way with any of those who had escaped. Aaron advised that on the day of the escape, he had been temporarily assigned to the shoe factory and that he had been formerly assigned to the clothing department, where inmate Will Green was assigned. He also confided that he knew inmate Curtis and that he had stopped by the first-aid room shortly before 9:00 a.m. seeking medicine for a cold. He stated Curtis was alone drinking coffee at the time. Afterward, he related that he went to the first floor and spoke with Officer Haag momentarily and spoke with inmate Green while returning to the third floor. Aaron said he spoke to Green about a young inmate who had just started in the clothing department and to break him in right—that he wanted to see the young inmate make good. Aaron claims to have gone back to the first-aid room and found it locked with the lights off. It was at this time that inmates began talking about the escape, stating that fifty men had gone out the front door. It was approximately 9:35 a.m., and as Aaron approached an office so that he could call the captain's office, he paused and saw officers running toward the administration building.

Aaron also stated that on December 13, he escorted a new inmate to the clothing department to be dressed in and that he spoke with Officer William Suberkrupt. At that time, Officer Suberkrupt approached and asked, "What can they do if a fellow gets in trouble?" Aaron asked what he meant and remarked, "You are not in trouble." Suberkrupt asked, "Did you ever give an inmate a key to the vault during the year you were in charge of the clothing department?" Aaron asked, "Have you let a convict have a key to the vault?" Suberkrupt's reply was "yes."

After interviewing inmates and speaking with Acting Warden Zerbst, Agents Lackey and Larimer visited with postmaster Ernest E. Brewster at the Leavenworth post office. It was discovered that Officer Carlson had rented P.O. Box 205 on December 4 with instructions that all mail addressed to him be placed in the box. A mail cover was placed on this box, and Brewster notified the agents on December 31 that the box had been released by Carlson.

On January 12, 1932, Brewster notified agents that a certified letter No. 29468—originating at Dallas, Texas—had been received the previous day and was addressed to C.A. Carlson, P.O. Box 205. It was scheduled for delivery to Carlson's residence at 205 Miami Street. Larimer and Lackey inspected the letter and noted that it contained currency and bore the return address of A.R. Barker, 5402 McComas Street, Dallas, Texas. An inmate by that name was currently at Leavenworth and had been received from Dallas, Texas. Lackey immediately notified the Dallas field office by phone. Agents in Dallas called upon the home of Mrs. A.R. Barker at the given return address. Mrs. Barker confirmed that she had mailed the registered letter to C.A. Carlson per her husband's instructions and that the letter contained a ten-dollar bill. She also confirmed that this had been the only letter to her husband that she had sent in this manner. The agents informed Zerbst of their findings, and two officers were assigned to observe Carlson.

On the morning of January 15, Carlson reported for duty and was assigned to tower No. 2, a small tower located directly in front of B cell house. During his shift, Carlson directed the warden's chauffeur, Lucious Clemons (No. 20433), to take a $10 bill and have it changed to specific denominations of paper and coins. Upon his relief from the tower, Carlson entered the institution and went straight to the officers' barbershop. Shortly thereafter, Clemons entered the shop and handed Carlson the following denominations: one $5 bill, two $1 bills, three $0.50 coins, five $0.25 coins, two dimes and one nickel. After leaving the barbershop, Carlson entered the gymnasium, where he found inmate James Venney (No. 33470). Carlson handed Venney $8.50 with instructions to pass the money to Barker. As Carlson was exiting the institution, agents, along with Warden Zerbst, apprehended him. Carlson was extensively questioned by agents and admitted to bringing in and taking out letters for inmates for a 15 percent fee of the total amount received per letter. A fee of $1 was charged each way for a letter containing no money. He continually denied any knowledge of the escape, handling any weapons or assisting with the escape in any manner. Carlson was immediately taken before U.S. Commissioner J.K. Codding in Leavenworth and charged with introduction of contraband within the prison. Carlson admitted his guilt to the commissioner and was ordered held in the Leavenworth County Jail with bond set at $7,500.

10

LOOSE ENDS

Early into the investigation, it had been decided by Special Agent in Charge Gus T. Jones that he would interview the surviving inmates, while Agents Hugh Larimer and Joseph Lackey would conduct the formal investigation. Jones first took the opportunity to view the inmates' files to see if there was anything that would give him an advantage. An interesting notation found in the file of Tom Underwood stated that he had only completed the second grade, had an IQ of 68 and had been classified as a "High Grade Moron." Tom Underwood and Stanley Brown had been placed in isolation cells in the segregation building, while Charles Berta and Earl Thayer had been placed in hospital annex No. 1.

Jones decided that he would conduct his interviews between the hours of midnight and dawn. During the initial interviews, Jones took the opportunity to size up Underwood and Brown to evaluate their individual personalities. He found Brown to be cynical in nature, taking a hard-line stance toward the interviewer. At first, Brown's only confession was that he had expected to be tortured in some fashion in order to make him talk. Underwood was the total opposite. He enjoyed boasting of his criminal exploits. After about the third night, both had become comfortable enough to share just about everything.

By the morning of December 17, Underwood had become so comfortable that he confided the following information: "From the very beginning, it was my understanding that this was George Curtis's party [referring to the inmate as Whitey]." Underwood claimed that Whitey had approached him about two months before and asked if he would be willing to take a chance on "going out." Underwood then stated, "Curtis saw me at the hospital annex No. 2 on the morning of the escape and told me I would have to make a decision at that moment if I would go. I told him I would go and that Curtis told me where to find the sawed-off shotgun." Agents encouraged Underwood to continue, and he did: "Curtis told me to go to the new construction area of the shoe factory by way of the south door and to make my way to the basement. Once there, I was instructed to go right and pass through a temporary partition and proceed to the north east corner of that room." Once in the room, Underwood found a pair of long underwear that had been cut up and tied together at the top and bottom. Inside, he found the Auto & Burglar shotgun and a bag of rounds. Underwood then stated, "Curtis told me that when I found the shotgun, I was to make my way to the main building, where two others would be waiting with forged passes."

Upon his arrival at the gate, Underwood was placed in the lead due to him wearing white clothes and working in the hospital. This allowed him to pass through the institution unchallenged. After making their way through the front gates, Underwood lamented, "After we failed to get the warden's Buick, we might as well turned back; the further we went, the more foolish the entire thing seemed to me. We were just like a bunch of chickens roaming around those muddy hills." He also stated that he felt Will Green had betrayed the others when he shot the warden.

In his report, Special Agent in Charge Jones stated that the bag Underwood described had been found during one of the mass shakedowns by Leavenworth lieutenant John C. Krautz. The bag was found in the plumbing room inside a piece of pipe, but nothing was thought of it until Underwood made his statement. The report also noted that the interviews of Stanley Brown had produced no tangible results and that Brown "prides himself on having always lived up to the prison code of not talking."

During one interview with Brown and Underwood, Jones decided to take a different approach. During a second shakedown of the plumbing room where Berta and Brown worked, officers found the remaining blasting caps and fuse hidden amongst sacks of concrete. The agent placed them on the desk in full view of Underwood and Brown. Over the course of the interview, the agent jokingly commented, "It's my job to find out how these weapons were smuggled into the institution, and it's your job to keep me from it." Jones continued with, "You know Uncle Sam is a patient old man, so don't feel that I am overstaying my welcome if I'm here this time next year." He watched their reactions.

The next evening, as the interview with Brown got underway, Jones tossed on the table the two telegrams the inmate had received. As Brown looked them over, Jones remarked, "Getting mighty close; I think we might find that empty barrel before long." In a fit of anger, Brown lost his composure for the first time, yelling, "You'll never find that barrel!" The agent replied, "Why you so sure?" Brown said, "Because I burned it; if the hoops will do you any good, you'll find them in the trash in the basement!" During the interview with Underwood later that evening, Agent Jones asked, "Why didn't you leave the shotgun in the original container instead of cutting up a pair of your drawers?" Coolly, Underwood replied, "I had to cut up those drawers because the tube the weapons were in was too conspicuous." Jones found it nearly impossible to contain himself as the interviews continued. Afterward, agents entered the area described by Brown and Underwood and were able to locate the three hoops. To their amazement, the hoops had not been burned and still bore stenciled lettering and red paint. They were also able to locate pieces of an inner tube.

During these interviews, both inmates identified the outside help as Fontaine, Nash, Holden and Keating. Brown claimed the escape was almost delayed twice because things had become "hot," and the outside gang was doing a lot of jumping around. When agents asked, Brown refused to elaborate, but agents concluded that the incident that led to the jumping around was the holdup of the Kraft State Bank on October 20, 1931, in Menominee, Wisconsin. It was known that Nash, Holden and Keating had pulled this job along with help from gangsters Charlie Harmon and Frank Weber. Weber had been Underwood's fall partner during a robbery that sent both to the Utah State Penitentiary. Underwood stated, "It's highly likely that Harmon and Weber had been murdered by Nash, Keating and Holden." During the getaway, Harmon had been struck in the neck by a bullet. As the crew made their escape, they took time to stop the vehicle and lay Harmon alongside the road, where he was later found dead. Also killed during the escape from the Kraft State Bank was a young man named James Kraft, son of the bank president, who was shot in the back of the head. Weber's body was found alongside Kraft having suffered a fatal gunshot to one of his eyes. Agents began to suspect that the three had also murdered Charlie Harmon's wife in Duluth, Minnesota, and buried her in quicklime.

Agents had attempted to interview inmate Berta but found him uncooperative. Inmate Thayer had confessed that he knew little about the escape or the involvement of others. A few days before the escape, Whitey (Curtis) confided in Thayer that there would be six inmates going out. Curtis confided that he had reservations about two of them, Berta and Green. Curtis feared that Green's high temper would lead to him doing bodily harm to the warden and others and that he had spoken with Green and told him he was to remain "cool-headed and do no violence." Green commented to Thayer on Berta being known as a bad man and that they were willing to take him but were not giving him a firearm. Thayer stated he told Curtis, "If there is to be no slaughter or if shooting or killing was going to be involved, he [Thayer] would not participate in the escape." Thayer claimed to have no knowledge of when the escape was to take place until December 9 and stated that on the morning of the escape, he met Curtis in the first-aid room, where he was handed the .30-30 rifle.

During the last interview, conducted on the night of December 28, inmate Brown finally admitted to Agents Jones, Larimer and Lackey that the entire escape was planned by Whitey Curtis and himself. The original plan had called for the outside help to ship the weapons into the institution hidden inside of an inner tube in the barrel of shoe paste. The morning of the escape, Nash, Keating and Holden, along with three others unknown to Brown and another individual he refused to name but whom agents believed to be George "Machine Gun" Kelly, were to come up the main drive in two separate cars—a Lincoln and a Cadillac, both equipped with police radios. They were to draw down on the officers in the main tower and open fire only if necessary.[44]

He admitted that he had approached inmate Ed Sherwood, who was rumored to be an expert getaway driver. Sherwood said he wasn't interested because he was serving his first sentence and was sure to make parole, but he recommended his fall partner Charles Berta. When asked about inside help, Brown asked, "Officers?" Larimer responded, "Yes, officers, especially Officer Carlson." Brown said, "Carlson can be reached—narcotics, liquor, mail can all be secured through Carlson." At the time of the capture of the escapees, a letter to inmate Phil Ryan had been found, and Brown had written the letter. The letter reads as follows:

> *Dear Pal Red,*
> *I don't wish you to think hard of me for not giving you a play. Wish I could old pal but this isn't my affair and I was asked to keep their confidence to myself and to only talk to the people that are only in the deal. Believe me, old side kick, I have slept very little of late thinking about you and Eddie not in but this is just one of those things as you call it. If it was my deal you would be first but it isn't so don't think any other way, old pal. The*

only reason Ollie got in is because of them wanting a driver and it was either Ed or Ollie and Ollie was given it by Ed. So you see how he must feel. But Phil there is seven in it and everyone seems to have someone so they decided to only take seven and that is the way it would stand. If we have success I will get in touch with you and Ed some way and if I can be of help I sure will be there. I talked to Danny and he said he could get anything regardless of what it is. Well Old pal wish me luck. No doubt plenty will put the hammer on me but that is to be expected. So long old pal.
[No signature.][45]

As the case began to come together, Agents Lackey and Larimer received word that Harold Fontaine had been taken into custody on January 19, 1932, in Windsor, Ontario, Canada, and was being held in the Sandwich Towne Jail. The FBI had advised Windsor police to be on the lookout for Fontaine and that he was a person of interest in the Leavenworth escape. Fontaine was taken into custody related to a 1926 arrest warrant that had never been served for an assault on a Michigan Central Railroad employee. During this time frame, Fontaine befriended a fellow inmate named Harry Mack, and over time, he confided key elements of the escape to Mack. What

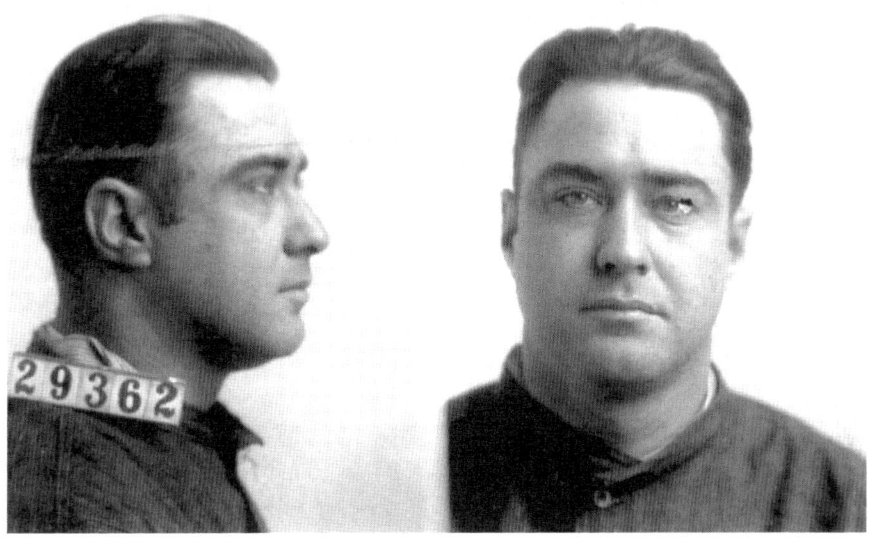

George Kelly Barnes, aka George "Machine Gun" Kelly, was an associate of Nash, Holden and Keating and thought to be the unidentified suspect involved in the escape conspiracy. *Courtesy National Archives and Records Administration.*

Fontaine hadn't realized is that inmate Mack was supplying this information to authorities. Mack later provided agents with a sworn affidavit that tied together the smuggling of the weapons.

The affidavit of Mack was completed and affirmed by agents on March 4, 1932, and provided the following information. Mack stated that since Fontaine had been arrested, they were housed in jail cells adjacent to each other and that in the beginning it was his opinion that Fontaine was talking just to gain publicity and attention.

As the weeks went by, Mack once again asked if Fontaine had really been involved, and that's when Fontaine confided the following information.

"Well Scotty, I will tell you how it was. You don't know how they do things to escape from a penitentiary." He went on to relate that he couldn't understand why some of his pals hadn't gone on the prison break, especially inmate Red Ryan, his former cell partner. Fontaine never named the other inmate but indicated that he was set up to receive and handle the barrel containing the firearms. He further stated that when he originally purchased the barrel of shoe paste, it was painted white, and they had to paint the barrel red to match the others sent to the prison. Mack stated that he laughed at Fontaine, asking, "Did you really purchase that barrel?" Fontaine's response was, "The first thing I done was send a telegram from Cicero on November 13th." He recounted that he had no fear of the telegram because there was nothing in it tying him to it. As the story continued, Fontaine admitted to purchasing the barrel and shipping it to Joliet, Illinois. Frank Nash and himself had picked up the barrel from the freight office and had placed it in a car. After driving for a while, they came to a neighborhood where he and Nash parted ways. Arrangements had been made by Nash for Fontaine to stay at a roadhouse in southern Illinois. Fontaine related that in the early morning hours of December 4, around 3:00 a.m., the owner of the roadhouse knocked on his door, telling him someone was downstairs asking for him. After dressing and going downstairs, he met with Nash, who asked, "Are you ready to go?" While Fontaine and Nash ate breakfast, Nash got up and walked outside. Upon his return, he handed Fontaine a .45-caliber Thompson machine gun, asking if the weapon was okay and if he had ever used one. Fontaine admitted that he had used one while in the military during the war.

After breakfast, the two got into the car, and after driving slow for a couple of miles, Fontaine asked Nash why they were going so slow. Nash pointed to a truck just ahead of them and told him that they were following that truck. Ahead of the truck, he could see a roadster leading the way. At approximately

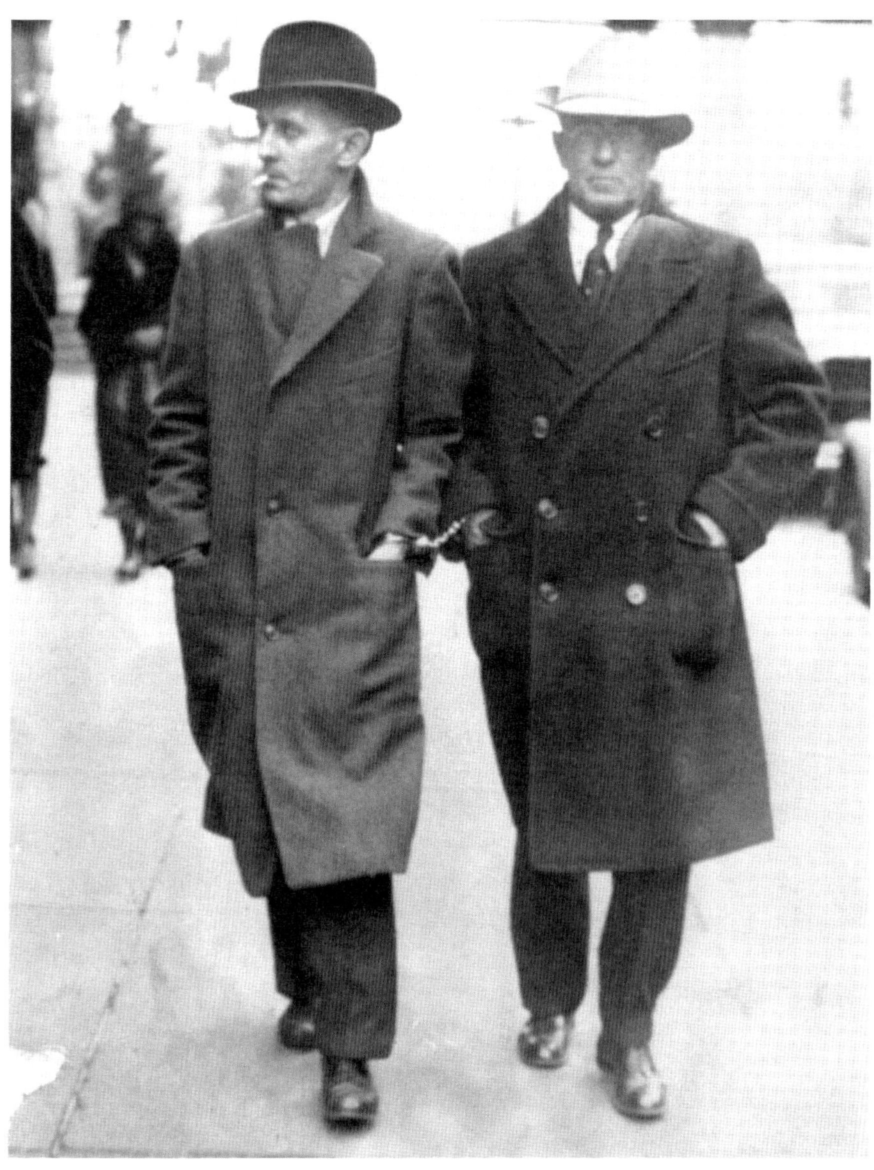

Harold "Monk" Fontaine (*left*) being escorted by an unidentified U.S. Marshal back to the jail in Kansas City, Kansas. Tired of his constant talking, Frank Nash made arrangements with the Boston mob to have Fontaine silenced. *Courtesy of the author.*

9:00 a.m., they arrived at a shipping office, where Nash stopped the car and told Fontaine to cover the truck and not let anything come between them. As he stood guard, he observed Thomas James Holden, Francis Keating and an unidentified man unloading the barrel and placing it upon the loading dock of the shipping office. He witnessed the unidentified man enter the office and later come out and get in the truck. At this time, the vehicles all separated, and Nash and he drove to the nearest Western Union office, where he sent a telegram. Fontaine said the telegram read, "Someone was very ill and leaving tonight."

From the time Fontaine was arrested on January 19, legal proceedings continued. Through appeals, delays, writs of habeas corpus and other legal issues, it was finally agreed that Fontaine was to be extradited back to the United States on May 20, 1932. Agents and Canadian authorities knew that Fontaine had been using his brother Earl, who was communicating with Nash about money needed for legal fees to fight the extradition. In late April, word had been received that no more money was to be sent. Fearing an escape attempt and a throng of news reporters, Special Agent R.D. Brown and U.S. Marshal Donald H. MacIver of Kansas removed Fontaine from the Sandwich Towne jail at 11:00 p.m. and drove across the Ambassador Bridge to the Wayne County jail, where Fontaine was booked under a different name. At 11:20 p.m. the following evening, Fontaine was removed from the jail and placed on a heavily guarded train bound for Kansas.

One of the biggest breaks to occur came on July 7, 1932. As agents were wrapping up the investigation into the escape, they received a tip that Thomas James Holden, Francis Jimmy Keating and Harvey Bailey were in the Kansas City area. All three were suspects in the Fort Scott Bank robbery that had occurred a few weeks earlier (on June 17). The trio came to town to receive their portion of the take along with Fred Barker, Larry DeVol, Alvin Karpis and Bernard Phillips. Agents had learned that Holden and Keating were golf enthusiasts and began checking the local courses. Witnesses at the Mission Hills Country Club identified Keating, Holden, Bailey and Phillips as being present playing a round of golf. While they were playing the eighth hole, agents apprehended three of the four unarmed suspects. At the request of Bureau of Prisons director Sanford Bates, Holden and Keating were sent to the federal prison annex on Fort Leavenworth. Bailey was turned over to Fort Scott authorities along with the Liberty Bond found on him that was taken during the robbery.

On July 22, Holden and Keating were interviewed by Special Agents Raymond J. Caffrey and B.F. Fitzsimmons. When questioned about

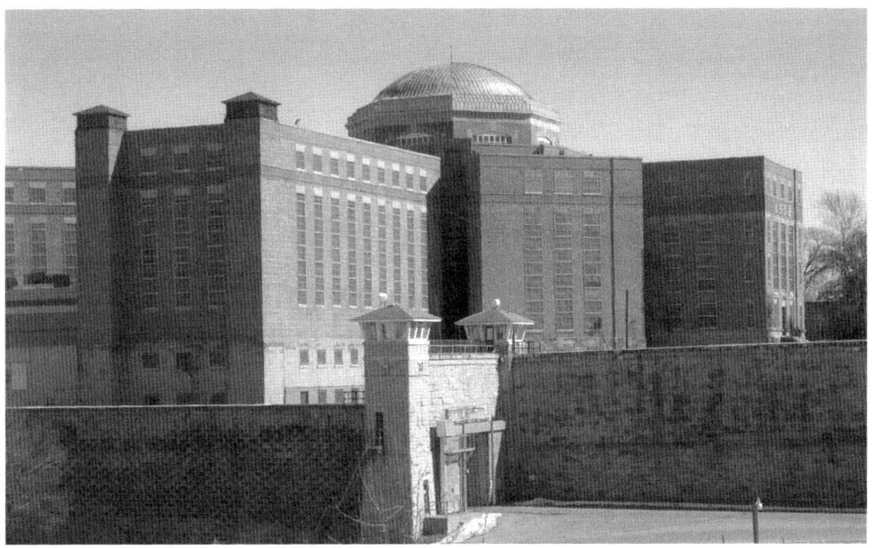

The old military prison on Fort Leavenworth is often confused with the federal prison. This was the site of the first U.S. Penitentiary from 1895 until 1904. The institution was turned over to the Department of Justice and operated as the Federal Prison Annex from 1930 until 1941, when it was returned to the military. *Courtesy of the author.*

their escape using trusty passes, Holden confessed that they had made arrangements for the passes with an inmate but refused to divulge his name or any additional information. During his interview, Keating confirmed the same but claimed the inmate who supplied the passes was now deceased. The two stories differed as to the events that occurred immediately following their escape. Holden claimed he immediately fled to Chicago, where he lived on Austin Boulevard under the name of Ripley. Keating claimed he proceeded to St. Paul, Minnesota, along with Holden, where they remained for four or five months. Afterward, both claimed to have bounced around, spending time in Montreal, Canada; South Dakota; Savannah, Georgia; Chicago and New York.

Both men were extensively questioned as to their part in the December 11, 1931, escape and their knowledge of Frank Nash. Holden and Keating both admitted to only knowing Nash as an acquaintance they met while at Leavenworth. Holden went on to explain that he had seen Nash several times around St. Paul. He further stated that he had a dislike for Nash and would not consider Nash in any venture whatsoever. When questioned about their knowledge of former inmate Harold Fontaine, both men denied having ever heard of or meeting him.

On July 26, 1932, Special Agents Caffrey and Fitzsimmons interviewed Fontaine at the Wyandotte County Jail in Kansas City, Kansas. At first, the suspect refused to speak with the agents, but he eventually agreed to an interview. Questioned about his exact whereabouts following his release, particularly from November 6, 1931, through January 1, 1932, Fontaine admitted that he returned to Windsor, Ontario, where he remained for about a week or two. He admitted to traveling to Cicero afterward and checking into the Annetta Hotel under the alias of James Murray. When asked about the telegrams sent to Stanley Brown and signed Margaret Brown, Fontaine remained noncommittal. In reply as to whether he had purchased the barrel of shoe paste and accompanied Nash, Holden and Keating to the Missouri Pacific freight office on December 5, Fontaine remained noncommittal. When asked by agents if he could provide an alibi that they were willing to investigate on his behalf, Fontaine remained silent.

HOTEL ANNETTA

CICERO, ILL.

Money, Jewelry and Valuables Must Be Deposited In The Office Safe, Otherwise The Proprietor Will Not Be Responsible For Any Loss.
GUESTS WITHOUT BAGGAGE ARE REQUIRED TO PAY IN ADVANCE

American Cabinet & Register Co., 2500 W. Lake St., Chicago, Ill.

MONDAY, NOVEMBER 30, 1931

NAME	RESIDENCE	TIME	ROOM
Ed S. Kerlin	Freeport Ill	5:40 A	339
[illegible]	" "		341
T. [illegible]	" "		338
Evelyn Frechette	Shebaygan		201
James Murray	Freeport	8:10 p.	208
R.L. Lee + wife	[illegible]	8:15 p.	101

During his interrogation, Fontaine was shown copies of the Annetta Hotel register dated from November 12 through December 4, 1931. Each page showed Frank Nash registered under the alias R.L. Lee and Fontaine under the alias James Murray. This page from November 30, 1931, also bears the signature of Evelyn Frechette, girlfriend of John Dillinger. *Courtesy of the author.*

During the interview of Fontaine, Special Agent Caffrey presented evidence provided by W.R. Hughes, manager, and W. Cargill, clerk, of the Annetta Hotel, both of whom positively identified Nash and Fontaine in photographs provided by agents from the Chicago field office. Also produced were photostatic copies of the hotel registry confirming that Nash had registered there under the name R.L. Lee and Fontaine under the name James Murray. Both were registered there from November 12 through December 4. Nash was again registered under the name R.L. Lee from December 5 through December 11.

EPILOGUE

Upon arriving at Leavenworth on the morning of December 12, Federal Bureau of Prisons director Sanford Bates met with investigators and prison officials. He also visited Warden Thomas White, who had undergone surgery the previous night at Cushing Hospital. Bates had come under heavy criticism from the press for his policy of complete secrecy regarding matters such as the escape. Nothing was to be leaked to the press until it was personally approved by him.[46] Since September 1931, the press had been seeking information about a foiled escape attempt that involved aviator Russell (Chesty) Hosler. Hosler, along with three other inmates, had constructed a glider atop the shoe factory that they were going to use to soar over the wall. The day before the escape was to happen, Hosler announced that the glider would only hold one inmate. The escape was foiled when the others who had assisted in the construction of the glider reported it to the warden. Further infuriating to the press was that Bates had stated he would speak to the press on the afternoon of December 17 in front of the prison. Upon arrival the members of the press were handed a piece of paper and advised that Bates had left for Washington. In part, Bates's statement read:

> *I cannot come to any other conclusion than the Warden Thomas B. White acted in a brave and resourceful manner and in the interest of the institution and its employees. The responsibility for the escape lies farther back. While responsibility cannot be definitely assigned to one individual there were several instances in which had a particular officer been a trifle more alert*

> *or resourceful or discriminating the whole regrettable affair might have been prevented. It seems almost incredible that seven men could possess themselves with firearms, gather together in a body and march out of an institution full of employees in the manner in which this was engineered. It must be admitted that there had grown up a laxity in the institution with reference to the issuance of passes to go and come in the various departments and that in some cases officers who should have assumed a more responsible attitude with reference to these inmates trusted in some other officer or agent to control them and that the presence of these prisoners at places other than where they were supposed to have been might well have been questioned and remedied.*

Bates also stated that there was no culpable negligence on the part of Hubert Gray (the armory officer) or Officers Dempsey and Kelly, who were held at gunpoint. "The last two of these officers was suddenly confronted with weapons at close range. Whether had they or the warden resisted the orders of the convicts their lives would have been sacrificed."

Upon reading the press release, officers became infuriated as well. Unsubstantiated reports led to as many as forty officers demanding transfers or resigning. Further complicating the situation was the December 20 suicide of Officer William Suberkrupt. The officer had worked what was known as the last half of the night shift and was relieved of duty and left the institution around 9:00 a.m. His wife reported that she last saw him alive shortly before leaving the house to go shopping. Upon returning home, she found his hat and coat in the house, but he was not to be found. Though his wife and family denied finding of a note, it was reportedly claimed that he left a note that read, "Goodbye, I can be found in the garage." After forced entry was made into the garage, the officer's body was found inside the car in a sitting position with the doors and windows closed. Coroner Ted Sexton concluded that Suberkrupt's cause of death had been asphyxiation due to carbon monoxide. Sexton also denied the presence of any note. Prison officials had quietly spoken about the comments made by Officer Leo Aaron during the investigation. It was also noted that on the day of the escape, Officer Suberkrupt was absent due to illness. Zerbst, other prison officials and investigators decided that a long-term illness was the reason for the suicide.

In her official statement and her statement to the press, Elizabeth Phillips, who was present when Warden White was shot, conveyed the following: "As we made our way across the field, the warden pleaded with the inmates, 'You aren't going to kill this girl are you? Why cause her to suffer?'" She stated that an inmate replied, "Well, we would kill you first anyway." After being ordered out of their car, Lyle Haite, Jack Gallivan and Carl Bauer began walking up the road as ordered to by inmate Green. Bauer looked over his shoulder and observed inmate Thayer pull up and level his rifle in their direction. Fearing they'd be shot, the three ran across Highway 92 and jumped into a ditch. From this vantage point, Haite and Gallivan stated, "we saw the warden wrestle with one of the inmates over a shotgun. At first, we thought that one of the inmates had fired from the rumble seat. The warden didn't fall immediately but staggered around for a few seconds and then fell into the ditch." The wounds Warden White sustained to his left arm were described by Dr. L.P. Engle. The shotgun charge entered two and a half inches below the elbow, with large patches of skin torn away at the entrance and exit of the charge. The muscles of the arm were badly torn, but the blood vessels were intact. Both bones were badly shattered in that portion of the arm, and several splintered pieces had to be removed. Enough of the remaining large pieces of the bone remained intact that doctors believed they would properly unite. Despite infection, the outlook was good for saving the arm.

On December 14, Warden White's wife, Bessie, gave an extensive interview to the *Leavenworth Times* in which she stated, "At one house, probably the Gates place, Tom had the opportunity to pick up a gun setting in the corner of the room when only one inmate was present; he had decided against taking the chance, believing it may have been a decoy." She further related that her husband hadn't spoken a complete sentence since being admitted to the hospital, that he had undergone a major surgery just a few weeks prior to the escape and had been forced to run on several occasions, which caused severe exhaustion. Bessie also spoke of the desperation of and a statement made by Earl Thayer to her husband, "This is the only chance I got, and if I die, you're gonna die with me."[47]

Another article appearing in the December 14 edition of the *Leavenworth Times* entitled "Guns Smuggled to Desperados in the Summer," as well as the FBI report, showed that a revolver had been found in C cell house the previous June. An outside company had been contracted to clean and repair the smokestack of the institution's powerhouse and received information that one of the outside workers had brought the weapon into the institution and given it to an unidentified inmate. In the same article and FBI report, it was disclosed that an unidentified officer had been arrested for introduction of contraband into the institution and had been extensively interrogated

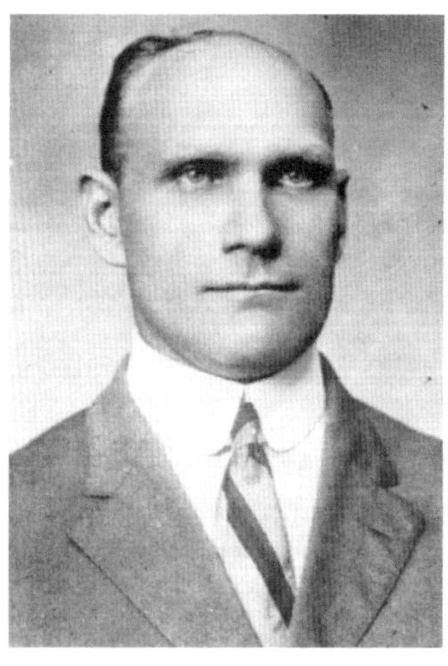

Fred G. Zerbst began his career at Leavenworth in 1897, starting as an officer and working his way up to warden, and experienced firsthand most of the institution's early history. *Courtesy of the author.*

during his time in the Leavenworth County jail. The former officer denied any knowledge of the revolver. As a result of that investigation, a door with a steel bar was placed across the foyer area leading to the dining room and auditorium area, and two additional doors, one on each side, had been placed on the east and west entrances to the main corridor at Leavenworth. Officers were instructed to pat search each and every inmate entering the main corridor area.

On Saturday morning, January 23, Officer William Brinson awoke around 6:00 a.m., as usual, and went about his normal routine. While on his way to work, he stopped by the home of his sister and brother-in-law (Martha and Antone Wolf) at 926 Pottawatomie Street. Placing two notes in the front door, Brinson knocked once and then stepped back before placing a revolver to his head and pulling the trigger. News of the officer's suicide came as a surprise to Acting Warden Fred Zerbst and staff of the institution. At no time had Brinson's name ever been brought up during the investigation. The first note, addressed to his sister and brother-in-law, read: "Take good care of Amanda, Good bye, Bill." The note addressed to his wife, Amanda, read: "Mandy, Goodbye, and may God forgive me. They framed me. I swear before God I did nothing wrong." An investigation was conducted, and one officer confided that Brinson, who was on duty in the east gate tower, had heard that the weapons and explosives had been smuggled in and hidden at the base of his tower until the day of the escape. The officer also stated that Brinson somehow believed the rumor and felt guilty for the events that occurred on the day of the escape. Bates, Zerbst and investigators moved quickly in their comments to the media, stressing that at no time was the officer suspected of any wrongdoing and that the suicide was caused by a long-term illness.

On February 6, 1932, Bates returned to Leavenworth to review the investigation with agents and prison officials. The following morning, Bates announced to the press that Warden Thomas B. White was being reassigned to the federal prison farm at El Paso, Texas, and that Fred G. Zerbst would assume the duties of warden of Leavenworth while Robert H. Hudspeth, former deputy warden of the Fort Leavenworth Prison Annex, would assume the duties of that institution's warden. Warden White's reporting date at El Paso was set for March 10, 1932.

On March 17, 1932, U.S. Assistant District Attorney Dan B. Cowie impaneled a grand jury at the federal courthouse in Wichita, Kansas. Forty-seven witnesses were called, evidence was displayed and the case was presented. The indictment included 114 separate counts, including attempted murder, introduction of weapons into a prison and escape. Tom Underwood, Stanley Brown, Earl Thayer and Charles Berta were found guilty of all 114 counts of the indictment. Harold Fontaine was also indicted on all counts, although his extradition from Canada had not been finalized. The affidavit of Harry Mack was presented to the grand jury as evidence providing proof of the participation of Frank Nash, Thomas Holden and Francis Keating; all three were also found guilty on all counts. Former officer C.N. Carlson was indicted on the charge of introduction of contraband. On April 11, 1932, Carlson entered a plea of guilty and was sentenced by federal judge Richard J. Hopkins to serve eighteen months in the state reformatory in Monroe, Washington.

On the morning of December 9, 1932, Underwood, Berta, Thayer and Brown—all of whom had filed writs of habeas corpus to stand trial separately—entered guilty pleas to the charges of assault with intent to kill, introducing contraband munitions in USP Leavenworth and escape from USP Leavenworth. Each were sentenced to five years per charge to run consecutively to their current sentences. Fontaine's trial began on the morning of December 8 and was given to the jury on the afternoon of December 9. The morning of December 10, Fontaine was found guilty and sentenced to twenty-five years. Holden and Keating both received sentences of five years to run consecutively to their earlier sentences of twenty-five years.

Following the sentencing of Holden and Keating, both men fully cooperated with investigators, providing information about the whereabouts of Nash. This information ultimately led to Nash's arrest on June 16, 1933, in Hot Springs, Arkansas. A few weeks before his arrest, Nash had orchestrated the escape of eleven inmates from the Kansas State Penitentiary. Once again, weapons were smuggled into the penitentiary, and a coded message sent by telegram to Wilbur "the Tri-State Terror" Underhill from his girlfriend stated, "Will cut hay on the thirtieth. Have purchased six cows at Picher, Oklahoma." The "cows" meant Underhill and his friends. The "hay" was the escape. The "thirtieth" meant Memorial Day, 1933.

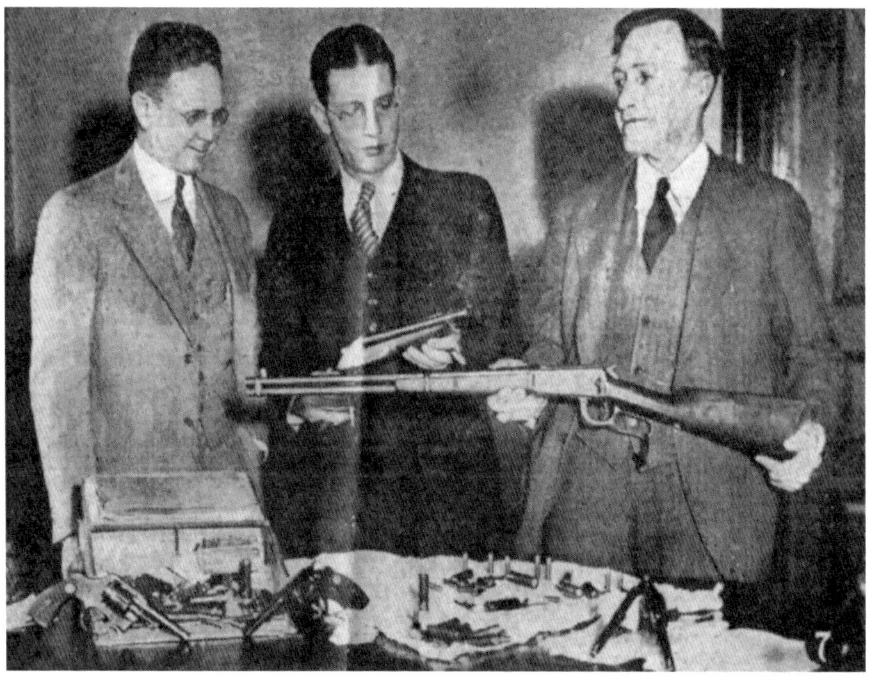

Left to right: Agent Hugh Larimer, assistant U.S. district attorney Dan Cowie and Agent J.B. Burger display the weapons, ammunition and explosives smuggled into the prison. *Courtesy of the author.*

During the fourth inning of a tied baseball game, Warden Kirk Prather was milling about the crowd when he came across Underhill. Prather immediately saw others with weapons and attempted to flee, but a gun was thrust into his stomach, followed by the order, "Come with us." As they headed toward three tower, more hostages were taken and more inmates joined in. At the base of the tower, the inmates forced Prather to order the tower officer to throw down his weapons and keys. As the hostage-takers ascended the tower, a rope made in the prison's twine factory was lowered. In total, eleven inmates escaped and three hostages were taken. From the very beginning, Underhill kept making threats to kill the warden. Harvey Bailey, who had been shot in the knee, prevented the murder. Bailey later stated, "I changed my mind on escaping only after learning Underhill wanted to kill the warden." The outlaws released Warden Prather and Officers John Sherman and L.A. Laws near Welch, Oklahoma. On June 17, Frank Nash was killed during the Union Station Massacre in Kansas City, Missouri.

The trials and convictions of all involved in the Leavenworth escape—along with the subsequent bank robberies, Lansing escape and Union Station Massacre—prompted the *Kansas City Journal Post* to run a five-weekend exposé from January 25 through February 17, 1935. Each weekend, the headlines were sensational, reading "Records Disclose Inside Story of Prison Breaks" or "Middle West is Barony of Crime after Prison Break." Inmate mugshots of criminals such as Frank Nitti, Machine Gun Kelly and Wilbur Underhill were pictured among copies of official inmate files and trusty agreements. Even though prison officials, as well as local and federal law enforcement, attempted to label the reports "yellow journalism," the stories contained quite a lot of detailed information.

Amongst the more than two thousand pages of the FBI report from which this story was crafted were the criminal profiles of each one of the escapees. Charles Berta had been committed to the St. Vincent Home for Boys in San Francisco at age ten. His extensive criminal career began as a juvenile with his arrest on December 16, 1919, by San Francisco Police for escape from a juvenile facility and theft of a horse and buggy. Under the alias of Harry Stone, Berta served time in Seattle and Tacoma, Washington. He was arrested on July 25, 1925, and extradited to Victoria, British Columbia, and charged with robbery with violence. He was sentenced to eight years and twenty lashes. After his release for good behavior, Berta was arrested and received twenty-six years for mail-train robbery. After serving time at McNeil Island in Washington, Berta was transferred to Leavenworth in November 1931. Tom Underwood was first arrested in 1919 for vagrancy in Denver, Colorado. From October 1919 until his arrival at Leavenworth in 1929, Underwood had served time for robberies in various institutions in Utah, Wisconsin, Minnesota, Iowa, Chicago and Memphis. During those incarcerations, he had served time under the aliases of Frank Devers, Bill Underwood, Frank Smith, Tom Smith and Pete Nolan. George "Whitey" Curtis (real name George Fallon) had served time in Oklahoma under the aliases Henry Ward and C.W. Curtis. Between 1916 and 1922, Curtis was charged with vagrancy, interstate shipment of liquor and robbery. Stanley Brown first served a two-year term at Leavenworth in 1919 for conspiracy to rob the mail train. In 1920, under the name Bernard McLaughlin, he was arrested in Sioux City, Iowa, for suspicion of holdup and safe-blowing. As Stanley Brown, he was arrested in Stillwater, Minnesota, for possession of burglary tools. Earl Thayer had served time in the Oklahoma State Penitentiary from 1913 until 1921 for automobile theft, burglary and grand larceny.

In September 1934, Holden, Keating, Berta, Underwood and Brown were all transferred to Alcatraz. All received notice of transfer on August 15,

1934, under transfer order No. 1747. Due to his age and medical condition, Earl Thayer died on July 28, 1934, at Leavenworth. Underwood and Brown returned to Leavenworth in 1942 to finish out their sentences. Both slipped into anonymity upon their release. Stanley J. Brown died on March 28, 1954, in Portland, Oregon. Francis L. (Jimmy) Keating was paroled in 1947. He returned to St. Paul, Minnesota, where he became president of the Boilermakers Union and a respected businessman. He passed away on July 25, 1978.[48] From the time he was paroled until his death, he never again saw Thomas Holden.

Holden was paroled in October 1947 and returned to Chicago. On June 6, 1949, Holden and his wife, Lillian, and Lillian's brothers John Archer and Ray Griffin and Ray's wife, Alva, had spent the evening barhopping to celebrate the birthday of Lillian's nephew, Joseph Grady. An argument between Thomas and Lillian began at a South Side tavern and continued on the way home. Once they were back at their apartment, Holden began to beat his wife, and when her brothers and sister-in-law came to her aid, Holden pulled a pistol and began shooting.[49] Lillian, John and Ray died at the scene. Alva, who was shot in the face and abdomen, underwent surgery at Inglewood Hospital and survived. Holden was last seen in Chicago in November that year as he fled police. During the investigation, it was discovered that Holden had pulled off several armed robberies prior to the murders. On March 14, 1950, Holden was the very first man ever placed on the FBI's newly formed Ten Most Wanted list. At the time, FBI director J. Edgar Hoover described Holden as a menace to every man, woman and child in America. Holden was taken into custody in Beaverton, Oregon, on June 23, 1951, following a tip from a citizen who had read an article in the June 20 edition of *The Oregonian*.[50] Upon his return to Chicago, Holden pleaded guilty to murder and was sentenced to life in prison. He died at the Cook County Jail on December 18, 1953.

Thomas White returned to Texas as the first warden of the new correctional institution at La Tuna. Officially opened on April 29, 1932, the institution received its first inmates on May 5 of that year. The institution was the Federal Bureau of Prisons' first meaningful effort at the rehabilitative side of corrections (as opposed to the punitive side). White embraced working with younger offenders as opposed to the older, more hardened offenders. White underwent additional surgery on his damaged left arm and never regained full use of it. During his tenure, White was instrumental in expanding the institution by adding staff housing, a bachelor officer's quarters, a dairy operation, farm buildings, modern livestock shelters and a 500,000-gallon in-ground water storage tank. On March 6, 1951, at age seventy, White retired after serving for nineteen years as warden of La Tuna. Upon his retirement, he accepted a position with the Texas Board of Pardons and Parole in Austin, where he worked for six years. Since his days as a railroad detective assigned to El Paso, Tom and his wife, Bessie, had always wanted to retire there. They returned to the city they loved in 1957 and built a home in the country club section of town. As a fully retired civilian, White enjoyed a weekly round of golf, his daily walks about town and participation in numerous civic groups. Thomas Bruce White passed away on December 21, 1971, at age ninety. His wife, Bessie, passed away on December 11, 1973. During his tenure as Leavenworth's warden, Tom White kept secret that the man who shot his brother John Dudley White in the back was an inmate at the facility.

Charlie Berta was released from Alcatraz in 1949. During the first couple of years on "The Rock," Berta was considered one of the hard-timers because of his constant disciplinary problems. Purportedly, he was the last inmate to serve disciplinary time in the infamous Alcatraz dungeon. Over time, Berta began to break and ultimately did his time as easily as possible. During the 1940s, he was assigned to a crew that welded buoyed netting for submarines used in World War II. Following his release, Berta found work in a local bar; legend has it he could look out the front windows of the establishment and see Alcatraz. Over the years, he had contacted Tom White and even visited with him during a trip to Texas. When Thomas White Jr. retired from the FBI, an agent in California told him that "Charlie Berta asks about your dad all the time and considers him one of the greatest men to ever live." On most afternoons, Charles Berta could be seen riding his bike across the Golden Gate Bridge, then sitting on a bench for hours staring at Alcatraz from across Aquatic Park. In an interview, a reporter asked him, "Why do you stare at Alcatraz for hours?" Berta's reply was, "That's where all my friends are."[51] The last surviving inmate from the December 11, 1931 escape, Charles Firmin Berta, passed away on December 16, 1989, at age eighty-seven.

NOTES

Preface

1. "Does It Pay to Escape Prison: Kansas Prison Break," *American Weekly*, 1934.
2. "Harry Pierpont: Biography," http://fampeople.com/cat-harry-pierpont.
3. John Neal Phillips, "Bonnie & Clyde's Revenge on Eastham," *American History*, October 2000. http://www.historynet.com/bonnie-clydes-revenge-on-eastham.htm.
4. FBI Records: The Vault, "Bonnie and Clyde," https://vault.fbi.gov/Bonnie%20and%20Clyde.

Chapter 1

5. Ralph Chaplin, *Bars and Shadows: The Prison Poems of Ralph Chaplin* (Great Britain, 1922).

Chapter 2

6. "The Finest of Penitentiaries," *Leavenworth Times*, March 21, 1897.
7. Leavenworth's first escape, June 5, 1898, official report of Warden James W. French, National Archives and Records Administration, Kansas City, Missouri.

8. Record of April 21, 1910 escape, warden's file (R.W. McClaughry), National Archives and Records Administration, Kansas City, Missouri.
9. "Escape of November 7, 1901," *Leavenworth Times*, November 8, 1901.
10. Letter sent on July 18, 1912, to James A. Finch, pardon attorney, by inmate Bob Clark (No. 4768), National Archives and Records Administration, Kansas City, Missouri.
11. "Desperate Plot Revealed," *Leavenworth Times*, December 19, 1901.

Chapter 3

12. Official FBI file of Frank Nash.
13. David Farris, "Last Train Robbery," *Edmond Life & Leisure*, March 9, 2017, http://edmondlifeandleisure.com/last-train-robbery-p14251-76.htm.
14. "Katy Limited Robbery: Eyewitness Account of Byron D. Tower," *Pawhuska Daily Capital*, August 21, 1923.
15. Paul I. Wellman, *A Dynasty of Western Outlaws* (Garden City, NY: Doubleday, 1961).
16. Letter to Mr. McDonald, *Pawhuska Daily Capital*, September 6, 1923.
17. David Farris, "Infamous Crook's Death Spurs Debate," *Edmond Life & Leisure*, March 23, 2017, http://edmondlifeandleisure.com/infamous-crooks-death-spurs-debate-p14330-76.htm.
18. Dixon et al. v. United States, 7 F.2d 818 (8th Cir. 1925).

Chapter 4

19. Verdon R. Adams, "WHITE, THOMAS BRUCE," *Handbook of Texas Online*, http://www.tshaonline.org/handbook/online/articles/fwh54.
20. Thomas L. Charlton, review of *Tom White: The Life of a Lawman*, by Verdon R. Adams, and *Texas Ranger Sketches*, by Robert W. Stephens (*The Southwestern Historical Quarterly*, Vol. 77, July 1973).
21. Sartain et al. v. United States, 16 F.2d 704 (5th Cir. 1927).
22. Patrick Millikin, "The Osage, Oil and the FBI," *True West*, https://truewestmagazine.com/osage-oil-fbi/.
23. Christopher Klein, "The FBI's First Big Case: The Osage Murders," History.com, April 24, 2017, https://www.history.com/news/the-fbis-first-big-case-the-osage-murders.

Chapter 5

24. Tim Nash, "Organized Crime in the 1920s and Prohibition," http://www.thefinertimes.com/20th-Century-Crime/organised-crime-in-the-1920s.html.
25. "W.I. Biddle Reappointed," *Leavenworth Times*, February 28, 1907.
26. Andrew Grant Wood, "Death of a Political Prisoner: Revisiting the Case of Ricardo Flores Magón," *A Contracorriente* 3, no. 1 (Fall 2005): 38, https://acontracorriente.chass.ncsu.edu/index.php/acontracorriente/article/view/127/52.
27. "Prisoner Runs Amok Killing Leonard and Wounding Six Others," *Leavenworth Post*, November 14, 1922.
28. "Wounds Fatal For Man Who Stabbed Captain Leonard," *Leavenworth Times*, November 30, 1922.
29. "Records Disclose Inside Story of Prison Breaks," *Kansas City Journal-Post*, January 25, 1935.
30. Donald G. Westlake, "The Hows and Whys of Prison Escapes," *Vice*, September 15, 2014.

Chapter 6

31. "Federal Prison Riot," *Leavenworth Times*, August 2–4, 1929.
32. "Parsnips and Prison Riots," *The Literary Digest*, April 19, 1930.
33. "Murder of R.G. Warnke," official reports of Officers Phil Holtgraves and Louis B. Guenther.
34. United States v. Carl Panzram, District Court of the United States, District of Kansas, First Divison, April 16, 1930, no. 5464.
35. "Execution of Carl Panzram, Inmate Number 31614," official inmate file, National Archives and Records Administration, Kansas City, Missouri.

Chapter 7

36. "Guns Smuggled Into Desperadoes in Summer," *Leavenworth Times*, December 14, 1931.
37. Official FBI report, December 11, 1931 Escape, FOIA request no. 1152436-000, January 31, 2011.
38. Narrative of Rose Haas Frietchen audiotape provided by Mary Alice Hund.

39. "Leavenworth Prison Break," *Kansas City Journal-Post,* December 12, 1931.
40. "Convicts May Have Been Under Spell of Dope," *Kansas City Journal-Post,* December 13, 1931.

Chapter 8

41. Official FBI report, December 11, 1931 Escape, FOIA request no. 1152436-000, January 31, 2011.

Chapter 9

42. Narrative of Rose Haas Frietchen audiotape provided by Mary Alice Hund.
43. "Leavenworth Prison Break," *Kansas City Journal-Post,* December 12, 1931.

Chapter 10

44. Mary Ann Jones, "The Leavenworth Prison Break," *Harper's Magazine,* July 1945.
45. Official FBI report, December 11, 1931 Escape, FOIA request no. 1152436-000, January 31, 2011.

Epilogue

46. Official FBI report, December 11, 1931 Escape, FOIA request no. 1152436-000, January 31, 2011.
47. Bessie White interview, *Leavenworth Times,* December 14, 1931.
48. Francis Keating family history, ancestry.com.
49. "Thomas James Holden Murder of Wife Lillian," *Chicago Tribune,* June 7, 1949.
50. "Fugitive Nabbed Near Beaverton," *The Oregonian,* June 24, 1951.
51. Charlie Berta interview, *San Francisco Chronicle,* 1954.

BIBLIOGRAPHY

Adams, Verdon, and R. Tom White. *Tom White: The Life of a Lawman*. El Paso: Texas Western Press, 1972.

Callahan, Clyde C., and Byron B. Jones. *Heritage of an Outlaw: The Story of Frank Nash*. Hobart, OK: Schoonmaker Publishers, 1979.

Chaplin, Ralph. *Bars and Shadows: The Prison Poems of Ralph Chaplin*. Great Britain, 1922.

Charlton, Thomas L. Review of *Tom White: The Life of a Lawman*, by Verdon R. Adams, and *Texas Ranger Sketches*, by Robert W. Stephens. *The Southwestern Historical Quarterly*, Volume 77, July 1973.

Cope, Jack. *1300 Metropolitan Avenue: A History of the United States Penitentiary at Leavenworth, Kansas*. 1960.

Edge, L.L. *Run the Cat Roads: A True Story of Bank Robbers in the 30's*. New York, W.W. Norton & Company, 1981

Gaddis, Thomas E., and James O. Long. *Killer: A Journal of Murder*. New York, Macmillan Company, 1970.

Grann, David. *Killers of the Flower Moon: The Osage Murders and the Birth of the FBI*. New York: Doubleday, 2017.

Jackson, Joe. *Leavenworth Train: A Fugitive's Search for Justice in the Vanishing West*. New York: Carroll and Graf, 2001.

Johnston, J.H., III. *Leavenworth Penitentiary: A History of America's Oldest Federal Prison*. Self-published, 2005.

Jones, Mary Ann. "The Leavenworth Prison Break." *Harper's Magazine*, July 1945.

Keve, Paul W. *Prisons and the American Conscience: A History of U.S. Federal Corrections*. Carbondale: Southern Illinois University Press, 1991.

Morn, Frank. *Forgotten Reformer: Robert McClaughry and the Criminal Justice Reform in Nineteenth-Century America*. Lanham, MD: University Press of America, 2010.

"Parsnips and Prison Riots." *The Literary Digest*, April 19, 1930.

Rudensky, Red. *The Gonif*. Piper Company, 1970.

Snyder, Martin (Editor). Leavenworth New Era: 50th Anniversary Edition, Federal Prison Industries, Vol. 18, Number 1–2, Summer 1964.

Weil, J.R. "Yellow Kid," and W.T. Brannon. *"Yellow Kid" Weil: The Autobiography of America's Master Swindler*. Chico, CA: AK Press/Nabat, 2011.

Westlake, Donald G. "The Hows and Whys of Prison Escapes." *Vice*, September 15, 2014.

Wharton, Charles S. *The House of Whispering Hate*. Chicago: M. Mendelsohn, 1932.

INDEX

C

D

E

F

G

H

I

J

K

L

M

N

O

P

Q

R

S

T

U

V

W

Y

Z

ABOUT THE AUTHOR

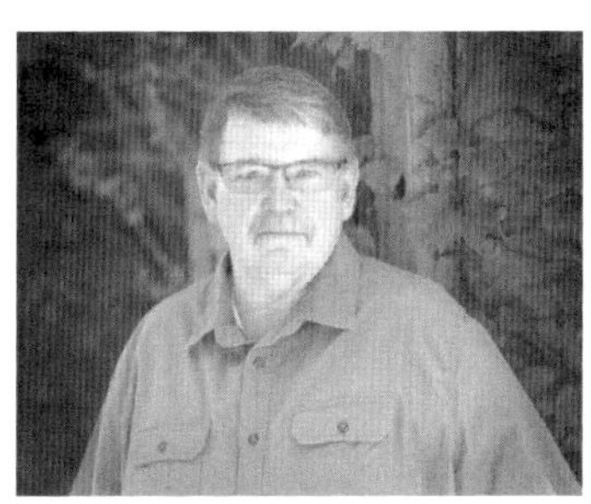

Courtesy Debra Bates-Lamborn, First City Photo and Frames, Leavenworth, Kansas.

Kenneth M. LaMaster is a retired correctional professional who worked at the U.S. Disciplinary Barracks at Fort Leavenworth, the Kansas State Penitentiary (now called Lansing Correctional Facility) and the U.S. Penitentiary, Leavenworth. His published works include three pictorial histories and numerous newspaper articles. As a guest speaker, he has appeared on C-SPAN's *Book TV* as well as in television and radio interviews. He has provided technical advisory work for television programs, documentaries and printed works by other authors. Originally from Louisville, Kentucky, he now resides in Leavenworth with Karen, his wife of thirty-six years.